ACCOUNTING PRINCIPLES

THIRD CANADIAN EDITION

ACCOUNTING PRINCIPLES

WORKING PAPERS

Part 1

Chapters 1-7

▶ **JERRY J. WEYGANDT** *Ph. D., C.P.A.*
Arthur Andersen Alumni Professor of Accounting
University of Wisconsin—Madison
Madison, Wisconsin

▶ **DONALD E. KIESO** *Ph. D., C.P.A.*
KPMG Peat Marwick Emeritus Professor of Accountancy
Northern Illinois University
DeKalb, Illinois

▶ **PAUL D. KIMMEL** *Ph. D., C.P.A.*
University of Wisconsin—Milwaukee
Milwaukee, Wisconsin

▶ **BARBARA TRENHOLM** *M.B.A., F.C.A.*
University of New Brunswick
Fredericton, New Brunswick

John Wiley & Sons Canada, Ltd.

National Library of Canada Cataloguing in Publication

Trenholm, Barbara A.
    Working papers to accompany Accounting principles, third Canadian edition / Barbara Trenholm.

ISBN 0-470-83458-7 (pt. 1).—ISBN 0-470-83459-5 (pt. 2)

    1. Accounting—Problems, exercises, etc. I. Title.

HF5635.A3778 2003 Suppl. 3   657'.044   C2003-907305-X

Production Credits
Publisher: John Horne
Publishing Services Director: Karen Bryan
Editorial Manager: Karen Staudinger
Senior Marketing Manager: Janine Daoust
Printing & Binding: Tri-Graphic Printing Limited

Printed and bound in Canada
10 9 8 7 6 5 4 3 2 1

John Wiley & Sons Canada, Ltd.
22 Worcester Road
Etobicoke, Ontario M9W 1L1

Visit our website at: www.wiley.com/canada

BE1-1

(a)

(b)

(c)

(d)

(e)

BE1-2

(a)

(b)

(c)

BE1-3

(a)

(b)

(c)

BE1-4

BE1-5

BE1-6	Assets	Liabilities	Owner's Equity
(a)			
(b)			
(c)			
(d)			
(e)			
(f)			

BE1-7

(a)		(f)	
(b)		(g)	
(c)		(h)	
(d)		(i)	
(e)		(j)	

BE1-8

(a)		(e)	
(b)		(f)	
(c)		(g)	
(d)		(h)	

BE1-9

(a)		(f)	
(b)		(g)	
(c)		(h)	
(d)		(i)	
(e)		(j)	

BE1-10

(a)		(f)	
(b)		(g)	
(c)		(h)	
(d)		(i)	
(e)		(j)	

E1-4

1	
2	
3	
4	
5	
6	

E1-5

Trans.	Assets	Liabilities	Owner's Equity			
			Owner's Capital	Drawings	Revenues	Expenses
1	+	NE	+	NE	NE	NE
2	–					–
3	+	+				
4	+ (AR)				+	
5	– (cash)			–		
6	+(cash) –(AR)					
7		– (AP)				–
8	–(cash) +(equip)					
9	+ (cash)				+	
10	– (cash)	– (AP)				

E1-6

Trans.	Assets			Liabilities	Owner's Equity			
	Cash	A/R	Equip	A/P	Capital +	Drawings −	Rev +	Exp −
1			+$19 000	+$19 000				
2	−$4000							−$4000 (rent)
3	+$15000	−$15000						
4	+$18 000						+$18 000	
5	−$11 000							−$11 000 (elec. bill)
6	+$32 000				+$32 000			
7	−$19 000			−$19 000				
8				+$1000				+$1000 (advert)
Total								

E1-7

Assets = Liab + Owners Equity

(a)

Cash	Supp. + A/R	Equip −	A/P	Capital	Draw	Rev.	Exp.
	$2450					$6100	
$3250	$760	$5000	$2050	$10 000	$-2000		$4200
	$9000						

(b)

(c)

E1-8

(a)	(e)
(b)	(f)
(c)	(g)
(d)	

E1-9

Name

Section

Date

Bourque + Co.
Income Statement
Month Ended Aug. 31, 2005

Revenue		
Service Revenue		$ 6100
Expenses		
Rent Expense	$ 750	~~750~~
Salaries Expense	2900	~~2900~~
Utilities Expense	550	~~550~~
Total Expenses		4200
Net Income		$ 1900

Bourque + Co.
Statement of Owners Equity
Month Ended Aug. 31, 2005

B. Bourque Capital, Aug. 1		$ 0
Add: Investment	$ 10 000	
Net Income	1 900	
		11 900
Less: Drawings		2000
B. Bourque Capital, Aug. 31		$ 9900

Bourque + Co.
Balance Sheet
August 31, 2005

Assets		
Cash		$ 3250
A/R		2950
Supplies		750
Equip		5000
Total Assets		$11 950
Liabilities & OE		
Liabilities		
- A/P		$ 2050
Owners Equity		
B. Bourque Capital		9900
Total Liab. & OE		$11 950

E1-12

E1-13

OTAGO COMPANY

Balance Sheet

December 31, 2005

E1-14 (a)

(b)

E1-15

Supporting Calculations	

(a)

Date	Assets		=	Liabilities	+	Owner's Equity		
Apr. 1								
2								
2								
7								
8								
11								
15								
25								
30								
30								
Total								

(b)

(a)

Date	Assets				=	Liabilities		+	Owner's Equity

(b)

(a)

(b)

(c)

(a)

(b)

(a)

(b)

(a)

(b)

GG Company

Balance Sheet

December 31, 2004

	General Journal			
Date	Account Titles and Explanation	Ref.	Debit	Credit

Cash	Service Revenue

Accounts Receivable	Salaries Expense

BE2-9

	Debit	Credit

BE2-10

BOURQUE COMPANY
Trial Balance
December 31, 2004

	Debit	Credit

Trans.	Account	(a) Normal Balance	(b) Decreased By	(c) Financial Statement
1	Accounts Payable			
2	Accounts Receivable			
3	Cash			
4	H. Poitras, Drawings			
5	Interest Revenue			
6	Office Equipment			
7	Prepaid Insurance			
8	Rent Expense			
9	Supplies			
10	Supplies Expense			

Trans.	Account Debited				Account Credited			
	(a) Basic Type	(b) Specific Account	(c) Normal Balance	(d) Effect	(a) Basic Type	(b) Specific Account	(c) Normal Balance	(d) Effect
Mar. 3	Asset	Cash	Debit	Increase	Owner's Equity	L. Visser, Capital	Credit	Increase
6								
7								
12								
21								
25								
28								
31								
31								

General Journal				
Date	Account Titles and Explanation	Ref.	Debit	Credit

	General Journal			
Date	Account Titles and Explanation	Ref.	Debit	Credit

Cash

Lynn Gardiner, Capital

Accounts Receivable

Fees Earned

Office Furniture

Salaries Expense

Accounts Payable

(a)

General Journal

Date	Account Titles and Explanation	Ref.	Debit	Credit

(b)

	Debit	Credit

E2-8 (a)

Cash	Notes Payable

Accounts Receivable	L. Meche, Capital

Office Equipment	Service Revenue

(b)

	Debit	Credit

E2-9

Section

Date

(a)

	Debit	Credit

(b)

(b) (Continued)

Account	(1) Type of Account	(2) Financial Statement	(3) Normal Balance	(4) Increase	(5) Decrease
				Debit	Credit
1. Cash	Asset	Balance Sheet	Debit		
2. A. Yee, Drawings					
3. Accounts Receivable					
4. Consulting Fees Earned					
5. Interest Expense					
6. Land					
7. Notes Payable					
8. Office Supplies					
9. Office Supplies Expense					
10. Salary Expense					

General Journal				
Date	Account Titles and Explanation	Ref.	Debit	Credit

(a)

General Journal

Date	Account Titles and Explanation	Ref.	Debit	Credit

(b)

Cash   No.101

Date	Explanation	Ref.	Debit	Credit	Balance

Accounts Receivable   No. 112

Date	Explanation	Ref.	Debit	Credit	Balance

Supplies   No. 126

Date	Explanation	Ref.	Debit	Credit	Balance

Office Equipment   No. 151

Date	Explanation	Ref.	Debit	Credit	Balance

Accounts Payable   No. 201

Date	Explanation	Ref.	Debit	Credit	Balance

Unearned Revenue   No. 209

Date	Explanation	Ref.	Debit	Credit	Balance

Section

Date

(b) (Continued)

Estella Rojas, Capital   No. 301

Date	Explanation	Ref.	Debit	Credit	Balance

Service Revenue   No. 400

Date	Explanation	Ref.	Debit	Credit	Balance

Salaries Expense   No. 726

Date	Explanation	Ref.	Debit	Credit	Balance

Rent Expense   No. 729

Date	Explanation	Ref.	Debit	Credit	Balance

(c)

	Debit	Credit

(a) and (c)

Cash

Date	Explanation	Ref.	Debit	Credit	Balance
Dec. 1	Balance				6,300

Accounts Receivable

Date	Explanation	Ref.	Debit	Credit	Balance
Dec. 1	Balance				1,800

Supplies

Date	Explanation	Ref.	Debit	Credit	Balance
Dec. 1	Balance				1,100

Equipment

Date	Explanation	Ref.	Debit	Credit	Balance
Dec. 1	Balance				16,000

Accounts Payable

Date	Explanation	Ref.	Debit	Credit	Balance
Dec. 1	Balance				5,250

Unearned Revenue

Date	Explanation	Ref.	Debit	Credit	Balance
Dec. 1	Balance				1,300

(a) and (c) (Continued)

Jane Cochrane, Capital

Date	Explanation	Ref.	Debit	Credit	Balance
Dec. 1	Balance				14,500

Jane Cochrane, Drawings

Date	Explanation	Ref.	Debit	Credit	Balance
Dec. 1	Balance				33,000

Laundry Revenue

Date	Explanation	Ref.	Debit	Credit	Balance
Dec. 1	Balance				64,900

Salaries Expense

Date	Explanation	Ref.	Debit	Credit	Balance
Dec. 1	Balance				11,525

Rent Expense

Date	Explanation	Ref.	Debit	Credit	Balance
Dec. 1	Balance				9,350

Utilities Expense

Date	Explanation	Ref.	Debit	Credit	Balance
Dec. 1	Balance				6,875

(b)

General Journal

Date	Account Titles and Explanation	Ref.	Debit	Credit

(d)

	Debit	Credit

(a) and (c)

Cash   No.101

Date	Explanation	Ref.	Debit	Credit	Balance
Mar-01	Balance				15,000

Accounts Receivable   No.112

Date	Explanation	Ref.	Debit	Credit	Balance

Land   No.140

Date	Explanation	Ref.	Debit	Credit	Balance
Mar-01	Balance				42,000

Buildings   No.145

Date	Explanation	Ref.	Debit	Credit	Balance
Mar-01	Balance				56,000

Equipment   No.157

Date	Explanation	Ref.	Debit	Credit	Balance
Mar-01	Balance				14,000

Accounts Payable   No.201

Date	Explanation	Ref.	Debit	Credit	Balance
Mar-01	Balance				12,000

Section

Date

(a) and (c) (Continued)

Unearned Admission Revenue   No.210

Date	Explanation	Ref.	Debit	Credit	Balance

Mortgage Payable   No.275

Date	Explanation	Ref.	Debit	Credit	Balance
Mar-01	Balance				65,000

L. Baroni, Capital   No.301

Date	Explanation	Ref.	Debit	Credit	Balance
Mar-01	Balance				50,000

Admission Revenue   No.405

Date	Explanation	Ref.	Debit	Credit	Balance

Concession Revenue   No.406

Date	Explanation	Ref.	Debit	Credit	Balance

Advertising Expense   No.610

Date	Explanation	Ref.	Debit	Credit	Balance

Film Rental Expense   No.632

Date	Explanation	Ref.	Debit	Credit	Balance

Salaries Expense   No.726

Date	Explanation	Ref.	Debit	Credit	Balance

(a) and (c) (Continued)

Interest Expense No.750

Date	Explanation	Ref.	Debit	Credit	Balance

(b)

General Journal J2

Date	Account Titles and Explanation	Ref.	Debit	Credit

(d)

	Debit	Credit

(a)

General Journal

Date	Account Titles and Explanation	Ref.	Debit	Credit

(b)

Cash

Date	Explanation	Ref.	Debit	Credit	Balance

Date	Explanation	Ref.	Debit	Credit	Balance

Date	Explanation	Ref.	Debit	Credit	Balance

Date	Explanation	Ref.	Debit	Credit	Balance

Date	Explanation	Ref.	Debit	Credit	Balance

(b) (Continued)

Date	Explanation	Ref.	Debit	Credit	Balance

Date	Explanation	Ref.	Debit	Credit	Balance

Date	Explanation	Ref.	Debit	Credit	Balance

Date	Explanation	Ref.	Debit	Credit	Balance

Date	Explanation	Ref.	Debit	Credit	Balance

Date	Explanation	Ref.	Debit	Credit	Balance

Date	Explanation	Ref.	Debit	Credit	Balance

(b) (Continued)

Date	Explanation	Ref.	Debit	Credit	Balance

Date	Explanation	Ref.	Debit	Credit	Balance

Date	Explanation	Ref.	Debit	Credit	Balance

Date	Explanation	Ref.	Debit	Credit	Balance

Date	Explanation	Ref.	Debit	Credit	Balance

Date	Explanation	Ref.	Debit	Credit	Balance

Date	Explanation	Ref.	Debit	Credit	Balance

Section

Date

(c)

	Debit	Credit

(d)

(d) (Continued)

Section _____
Date _____

(a)

(b) and (d)   Cash

Date	Explanation	Ref.	Debit	Credit	Balance
Jan. 1	Balance				2,000

Accounts Receivable

Date	Explanation	Ref.	Debit	Credit	Balance
Jan. 1	Balance				15,000

Repair Parts Inventory

Date	Explanation	Ref.	Debit	Credit	Balance
Jan. 1	Balance				13,000

Prepaid Rent

Date	Explanation	Ref.	Debit	Credit	Balance
Jan. 1	Balance				2,800

(b) (Continued)

Shop Equipment

Date	Explanation	Ref.	Debit	Credit	Balance
Jan. 1	Balance				24,000

Accounts Payable

Date	Explanation	Ref.	Debit	Credit	Balance
Jan. 1	Balance				19,000

Leo Mataruka, Capital

Date	Explanation	Ref.	Debit	Credit	Balance
Jan. 1	Balance				37,800

Date		Ref.	Debit	Credit	Balance

Date		Ref.	Debit	Credit	Balance

Date		Ref.	Debit	Credit	Balance

(b) (Continued)

Date		Ref.	Debit	Credit	Balance

Date		Ref.	Debit	Credit	Balance

Date		Ref.	Debit	Credit	Balance

Date		Ref.	Debit	Credit	Balance

Date		Ref.	Debit	Credit	Balance

Date		Ref.	Debit	Credit	Balance

Date		Ref.	Debit	Credit	Balance

(c)

General Journal

Date	Account Titles and Explanation	Ref.	Debit	Credit

(e)

	Debit	Credit

(f)

(g)

(a)

(b)

(c)

(d)

Section _____

Date _____

(a)

(b)

Trans.	1	2	3	4	5
1					
2					
3					
4					
5					
6					
7					
8					

WINAU CO. Trial Balance June 30, 2005		
	Debit	Credit

Account	(1) Type of Account	(2) Financial Statement	(3) Normal Balance	(4) Increase	(5) Decrease
1. Cash	Asset	Balance Sheet	Debit	Debit	Credit
2. M. Kobayashi, Capital					
3. Accounts Payable					
4. Building					
5. Consulting Fee Revenue					
6. Insurance Expense					
7. Interest Earned					
8. Notes Receivable					
9. Prepaid Insurance					
10. Rent Expense					
11. Unearned Consulting Fees					

	General Journal			
Date	Account Titles and Explanation	Ref.	Debit	Credit

(a) and (c) (Continued)

Accounts Payable

Date	Explanation	Ref.	Debit	Credit	Balance
Jul-01	Balance				13,066

Unearned Revenue

Date	Explanation	Ref.	Debit	Credit	Balance
Jul-01	Balance				1,920

Note Payable

Date	Explanation	Ref.	Debit	Credit	Balance

E. Brisebois, Capital

Date	Explanation	Ref.	Debit	Credit	Balance
Jul-01	Balance				51,920

E. Brisebois, Drawings

Date	Explanation	Ref.	Debit	Credit	Balance
Jul-01	Balance				39,050

Dry Cleaning Revenue

Date	Explanation	Ref.	Debit	Credit	Balance
Jul-01	Balance				109,461

(a) and (c) (Continued)

Interest Revenue

Date	Explanation	Ref.	Debit	Credit	Balance

Salaries Expense

Date	Explanation	Ref.	Debit	Credit	Balance
Jul-01	Balance				57,750

Rent Expense

Date	Explanation	Ref.	Debit	Credit	Balance
Jul-01	Balance				11,385

Repair Expense

Date	Explanation	Ref.	Debit	Credit	Balance
Jul-01	Balance				1,727

Utilities Expense

Date	Explanation	Ref.	Debit	Credit	Balance
Jul-01	Balance				14,520

(b)

General Journal   J1

Date	Account Titles and Explanation	Ref.	Debit	Credit

(d)

	Debit	Credit

(a) and (c)

Cash

Date	Explanation	Ref.	Debit	Credit	Balance
Apr-01	Balance				6,000

Accounts Receivable

Date	Explanation	Ref.	Debit	Credit	Balance

Prepaid Rentals

Date	Explanation	Ref.	Debit	Credit	Balance

Land

Date	Explanation	Ref.	Debit	Credit	Balance
Apr-01	Balance				40,000

Buildings

Date	Explanation	Ref.	Debit	Credit	Balance
Apr-01	Balance				60,000

Equipment

Date	Explanation	Ref.	Debit	Credit	Balance
Apr-01	Balance				16,000

(a) and (c) (Continued)

Unearned Admissions Revenue

Date	Explanation	Ref.	Debit	Credit	Balance

Accounts Payable

Date	Explanation	Ref.	Debit	Credit	Balance
Apr-01	Balance				4,000

Mortgage Payable

Date	Explanation	Ref.	Debit	Credit	Balance
Apr-01	Balance				80,000

Fran Goresht, Capital

Date	Explanation	Ref.	Debit	Credit	Balance

Date	Explanation	Ref.	Debit	Credit	Balance

Date	Explanation	Ref.	Debit	Credit	Balance

(a) and (c) (Continued)

Date	Explanation	Ref.	Debit	Credit	Balance

Date	Explanation	Ref.	Debit	Credit	Balance

Date	Explanation	Ref.	Debit	Credit	Balance

Date	Explanation	Ref.	Debit	Credit	Balance

Date	Explanation	Ref.	Debit	Credit	Balance

Date	Explanation	Ref.	Debit	Credit	Balance

Date	Explanation	Ref.	Debit	Credit	Balance

(b)

General Journal

Date	Account Titles and Explanation	Ref.	Debit	Credit

(d)

	Debit	Credit

(a)

General Journal

Date	Account Titles and Explanation	Ref.	Debit	Credit

(b)

Cash

Date	Explanation	Ref.	Debit	Credit	Balance

Date	Explanation	Ref.	Debit	Credit	Balance

Date	Explanation	Ref.	Debit	Credit	Balance

Date	Explanation	Ref.	Debit	Credit	Balance

(b) (Continued)

Date	Explanation	Ref.	Debit	Credit	Balance

Date	Explanation	Ref.	Debit	Credit	Balance

Date	Explanation	Ref.	Debit	Credit	Balance

Date	Explanation	Ref.	Debit	Credit	Balance

Date	Explanation	Ref.	Debit	Credit	Balance

Date	Explanation	Ref.	Debit	Credit	Balance

(b) (Continued)

Date	Explanation	Ref.	Debit	Credit	Balance

Date	Explanation	Ref.	Debit	Credit	Balance

Date	Explanation	Ref.	Debit	Credit	Balance

Date	Explanation	Ref.	Debit	Credit	Balance

Date	Explanation	Ref.	Debit	Credit	Balance

Date	Explanation	Ref.	Debit	Credit	Balance

Section

Date

(c)

	Debit	Credit

(d)

(a)

(b)

(c)

(d)

(a)

(b)

Trans.	1	2	3	4	5
1					
2					
3					
4					
5					
6					
7					
8					

SHAWNEE COMPANY		
Trial Balance		
May 31, 2005		
	Debit	Credit

(b) (Continued)

Date	Explanation	Ref.	Debit	Credit	Balance

Date	Explanation	Ref.	Debit	Credit	Balance

Date	Explanation	Ref.	Debit	Credit	Balance

Date	Explanation	Ref.	Debit	Credit	Balance

Date	Explanation	Ref.	Debit	Credit	Balance

Date	Explanation	Ref.	Debit	Credit	Balance

Date	Explanation	Ref.	Debit	Credit	Balance

(c)

	Debit	Credit

(a) and (b)

General Journal

Date	Account Titles and Explanation	Ref.	Debit	Credit

(a) to (c)

(a) and (b)

General Journal

Date	Account Titles and Explanation	Ref.	Debit	Credit

(b) (Continued)

Accumulated Amortization - Buses

Date	Explanation	Ref.	Debit	Credit	Balance
June 30	Balance				46,800

Notes Payable

Date	Explanation	Ref.	Debit	Credit	Balance
June 30	Balance				54,000

Accounts Payable

Date	Explanation	Ref.	Debit	Credit	Balance
June 30	Balance				1,985

Interest Payable

Date	Explanation	Ref.	Debit	Credit	Balance

Salaries Payable

Date	Explanation	Ref.	Debit	Credit	Balance

Unearned Fees

Date	Explanation	Ref.	Debit	Credit	Balance
June 30	Balance				14,000

Eldon Kaplan, Capital

Date	Explanation	Ref.	Debit	Credit	Balance
June 30	Balance				45,000

(b) (Continued)

Eldon Kaplan, Drawings

Date	Explanation	Ref.	Debit	Credit	Balance
June 30	Balance				3,400

Fees Earned

Date	Explanation	Ref.	Debit	Credit	Balance
June 30	Balance				17,110

Salaries Expense

Date	Explanation	Ref.	Debit	Credit	Balance
June 30	Balance				9,560

Advertising Expense

Date	Explanation	Ref.	Debit	Credit	Balance
June 30	Balance				825

Rent Expense

Date	Explanation	Ref.	Debit	Credit	Balance
June 30	Balance				2,175

Gas and Oil Expense

Date	Explanation	Ref.	Debit	Credit	Balance
June 30	Balance				1,170

Name

Section

Date

(b) (Continued)

Date	Explanation	Ref.	Debit	Credit	Balance

Date	Explanation	Ref.	Debit	Credit	Balance

Date	Explanation	Ref.	Debit	Credit	Balance

Date	Explanation	Ref.	Debit	Credit	Balance

Date	Explanation	Ref.	Debit	Credit	Balance

Date	Explanation	Ref.	Debit	Credit	Balance

Date	Explanation	Ref.	Debit	Credit	Balance

(c)

	Debit	Credit

(a)

General Journal

Date	Account Titles and Explanation	Ref.	Debit	Credit

(b)

Cash

Date	Explanation	Ref.	Debit	Credit	Balance
Aug. 31	Balance				18,870

Accounts Receivable

Date	Explanation	Ref.	Debit	Credit	Balance

Prepaid Insurance

Date	Explanation	Ref.	Debit	Credit	Balance
Aug. 31	Balance				6,360

Supplies

Date	Explanation	Ref.	Debit	Credit	Balance
Aug. 31	Balance				3,495

Land

Date	Explanation	Ref.	Debit	Credit	Balance
Aug. 31	Balance				25,000

Cottages

Date	Explanation	Ref.	Debit	Credit	Balance
Aug. 31	Balance				145,000

Accumulated Amortization - Cottages

Date	Explanation	Ref.	Debit	Credit	Balance
Aug. 31	Balance				34,800

(b) (Continued)

Furniture

Date	Explanation	Ref.	Debit	Credit	Balance
Aug. 31	Balance				28,600

Accumulated Amortization - Furniture

Date	Explanation	Ref.	Debit	Credit	Balance
Aug. 31	Balance				10,725

Accounts Payable

Date	Explanation	Ref.	Debit	Credit	Balance
Aug. 31	Balance				6,500

Uneaened Rent Revenue

Date	Explanation	Ref.	Debit	Credit	Balance
Aug. 31	Balance				36,200

Salaries Payable

Date	Explanation	Ref.	Debit	Credit	Balance

Interest Payable

Date	Explanation	Ref.	Debit	Credit	Balance

Mortgage Payable

Date	Explanation	Ref.	Debit	Credit	Balance
Aug. 31	Balance				60,000

(b) (Continued)

Keath Yhap, Capital

Date	Explanation	Ref.	Debit	Credit	Balance
Aug. 31	Balance				85,000

Keath Yhap, Drawings

Date	Explanation	Ref.	Debit	Credit	Balance
Aug. 31	Balance				44,000

Rent Revenue

Date	Explanation	Ref.	Debit	Credit	Balance
Aug. 31	Balance				247,500

Salaries Expense

Date	Explanation	Ref.	Debit	Credit	Balance
Aug. 31	Balance				153,000

Interest Expense

Date	Explanation	Ref.	Debit	Credit	Balance
Aug. 31	Balance				4,400

Utilities Expense

Date	Explanation	Ref.	Debit	Credit	Balance
Aug. 31	Balance				37,600

Repair Expense

Date	Explanation	Ref.	Debit	Credit	Balance
Aug. 31	Balance				14,400

(b) (Continued)

Date	Explanation	Ref.	Debit	Credit	Balance

Date	Explanation	Ref.	Debit	Credit	Balance

Date	Explanation	Ref.	Debit	Credit	Balance

Date	Explanation	Ref.	Debit	Credit	Balance

Date	Explanation	Ref.	Debit	Credit	Balance

Date	Explanation	Ref.	Debit	Credit	Balance

Date	Explanation	Ref.	Debit	Credit	Balance

(c)

	Debit	Credit

(d)

(d) (Continued)

(a)

General Journal

Date	Account Titles and Explanation	Ref.	Debit	Credit

(b)

(b) (Continued)

(c) and (d)

(a)

General Journal

Date	Account Titles and Explanation	Ref.	Debit	Credit

(b)

	Debit	Credit

(c)

(c) (Continued) and (d)

	General Journal			
Date	Account Titles and Explanation	Ref.	Debit	Credit

(b)

	Debit	Credit

(c)

(b) (Continued)

Office Furniture

Date	Explanation	Ref.	Debit	Credit	Balance
Dec.31	Balance				16,000

Accumulated Amortization - Office Furniture

Date	Explanation	Ref.	Debit	Credit	Balance
Dec.31	Balance				4,000

Notes Payable

Date	Explanation	Ref.	Debit	Credit	Balance
Dec.31	Balance				46,000

Unearned Revenue

Date	Explanation	Ref.	Debit	Credit	Balance
Dec.31					3,600

Interest Payable

Date	Explanation	Ref.	Debit	Credit	Balance

Salaries Payable

Date	Explanation	Ref.	Debit	Credit	Balance

C. Orosco, Capital

Date	Explanation	Ref.	Debit	Credit	Balance
Dec.31	Balance				56,000

(b) (Continued)

C. Orosco, Drawings

Date	Explanation	Ref.	Debit	Credit	Balance
Dec.31	Balance				38,400

Service Revenue

Date	Explanation	Ref.	Debit	Credit	Balance
Dec.31	Balance				101,605

Salaries Expense

Date	Explanation	Ref.	Debit	Credit	Balance
Dec.31	Balance				57,000

Interest Expense

Date	Explanation	Ref.	Debit	Credit	Balance
Dec.31	Balance				3,105

Rent Expense

Date	Explanation	Ref.	Debit	Credit	Balance
Dec.31	Balance				14,700

Repair Expense

Date	Explanation	Ref.	Debit	Credit	Balance
Dec.31	Balance				6,000

Gas and Oil Expense

Date	Explanation	Ref.	Debit	Credit	Balance
Dec.31	Balance				9,300

(b) (Continued)

Date	Explanation	Ref.	Debit	Credit	Balance

Date	Explanation	Ref.	Debit	Credit	Balance

Date	Explanation	Ref.	Debit	Credit	Balance

Date	Explanation	Ref.	Debit	Credit	Balance

Date	Explanation	Ref.	Debit	Credit	Balance

Date	Explanation	Ref.	Debit	Credit	Balance

Date	Explanation	Ref.	Debit	Credit	Balance

(c)

	Debit	Credit

(a)

General Journal

Date	Account Titles and Explanation	Ref.	Debit	Credit

(b)

Cash

Date	Explanation	Ref.	Debit	Credit	Balance
May 31	Balance				2,200

Accounts Receivable

Date	Explanation	Ref.	Debit	Credit	Balance

Prepaid Insurance

Date	Explanation	Ref.	Debit	Credit	Balance
May 31	Balance				5,460

Supplies

Date	Explanation	Ref.	Debit	Credit	Balance
May 31	Balance				2,440

Land

Date	Explanation	Ref.	Debit	Credit	Balance
May 31	Balance				30,000

Lodge

Date	Explanation	Ref.	Debit	Credit	Balance
May 31	Balance				84,000

Accumulated Amortization - Lodge

Date	Explanation	Ref.	Debit	Credit	Balance
May 31	Balance				29,400

(b) (Continued)

Furniture

Date	Explanation	Ref.	Debit	Credit	Balance
May 31	Balance				17,200

Accumulated Amortization - Furniture

Date	Explanation	Ref.	Debit	Credit	Balance
May 31	Balance				6,880

Accounts Payable

Date	Explanation	Ref.	Debit	Credit	Balance
May 31	Balance				4,700

Uneaened Rent Revenue

Date	Explanation	Ref.	Debit	Credit	Balance
May 31	Balance				8,750

Salaries Payable

Date	Explanation	Ref.	Debit	Credit	Balance

Interest Payable

Date	Explanation	Ref.	Debit	Credit	Balance

Mortgage Payable

Date	Explanation	Ref.	Debit	Credit	Balance
May 31	Balance				63,000

(b) (Continued)

Sara Sutton, Capital

Date	Explanation	Ref.	Debit	Credit	Balance
May 31	Balance				30,500

Sara Sutton, Drawings

Date	Explanation	Ref.	Debit	Credit	Balance
May 31	Balance				33,500

Rent Revenue

Date	Explanation	Ref.	Debit	Credit	Balance
May 31	Balance				101,160

Salaries Expense

Date	Explanation	Ref.	Debit	Credit	Balance
May 31	Balance				49,350

Interest Expense

Date	Explanation	Ref.	Debit	Credit	Balance
May 31	Balance				4,620

Insurance Expense

Date	Explanation	Ref.	Debit	Credit	Balance
May 31	Balance				1,820

Utilities Expense

Date	Explanation	Ref.	Debit	Credit	Balance
May 31	Balance				13,300

(b) (Continued)

Advertising Expense

Date	Explanation	Ref.	Debit	Credit	Balance
May 31	Balance				500

Date	Explanation	Ref.	Debit	Credit	Balance

Date	Explanation	Ref.	Debit	Credit	Balance

Date	Explanation	Ref.	Debit	Credit	Balance

Date	Explanation	Ref.	Debit	Credit	Balance

Date	Explanation	Ref.	Debit	Credit	Balance

Date	Explanation	Ref.	Debit	Credit	Balance

(c)

	Debit	Credit

(d)

(d) (Continued)

(a)

General Journal

Date	Account Titles and Explanation	Ref.	Debit	Credit

(b)

(b) (Continued)

(c) and (d)

(a)

General Journal

Date	Account Titles and Explanation	Ref.	Debit	Credit

(b)

	Debit	Credit

(c)

(c) (Continued)

General Journal				
Date	Account Titles and Explanation	Ref.	Debit	Credit

(b)

	Debit	Credit

(c)

(c) (Continued)

(a)

General Journal

Date	Account Titles and Explanation	Ref.	Debit	Credit

Cash

Date	Explanation	Ref.	Debit	Credit	Balance
Nov. 30	Unadjusted balance				305

Accounts Receivable

Date	Explanation	Ref.	Debit	Credit	Balance

Advertising Supplies

Date	Explanation	Ref.	Debit	Credit	Balance
Nov. 30	Unadjusted balance				95

Baking Supplies

Date	Explanation	Ref.	Debit	Credit	Balance
Nov. 30	Unadjusted balance				125

Prepaid Insurance

Date	Explanation	Ref.	Debit	Credit	Balance
Nov. 30	Unadjusted balance				1,200

Baking Equipment

Date	Explanation	Ref.	Debit	Credit	Balance
Nov. 30	Unadjusted balance				1,200

Accumulated Amortization - Baking Equipment

Date	Explanation	Ref.	Debit	Credit	Balance

(a) (Continued)

Website

Date	Explanation	Ref.	Debit	Credit	Balance
Nov. 30	Unadjusted balance				600

Accounts Payable

Date	Explanation	Ref.	Debit	Credit	Balance
Nov. 30	Unadjusted balance				600

Interest Payable

Date	Explanation	Ref.	Debit	Credit	Balance

Unearned Revenue

Date	Explanation	Ref.	Debit	Credit	Balance
Nov. 30	Unadjusted balance				25

Notes Payable

Date	Explanation	Ref.	Debit	Credit	Balance
Nov. 30	Unadjusted balance				2,000

N. Koebel, Capital

Date	Explanation	Ref.	Debit	Credit	Balance
Nov. 30	Unadjusted balance				800

Teaching Revenue

Date	Explanation	Ref.	Debit	Credit	Balance
Nov. 30	Unadjusted balance				100

Name _____

Section _____

Date _____

(a), (c), and (e)

Cash

Date	Explanation	Ref.	Debit	Credit	Balance
Sept. 1	Balance				4,880

Accounts Receivable

Date	Explanation	Ref.	Debit	Credit	Balance
Sept. 1	Balance				3,720

Supplies

Date	Explanation	Ref.	Debit	Credit	Balance
Sept. 1	Balance				800

Store Equipment

Date	Explanation	Ref.	Debit	Credit	Balance
Sept. 1	Balance				15,000

Accumulated Amortization - Store Equipment

Date	Explanation	Ref.	Debit	Credit	Balance
Sept. 1	Balance				1,500

(a), (c), and (e) (Continued)

Accounts Payable

Date	Explanation	Ref.	Debit	Credit	Balance
Sept. 1	Balance				3,100

Unearned Service Revenue

Date	Explanation	Ref.	Debit	Credit	Balance
Sept. 1	Balance				400

Salaries Payable

Date	Explanation	Ref.	Debit	Credit	Balance
Sept. 1	Balance				700

R. Pitre, Capital

Date	Explanation	Ref.	Debit	Credit	Balance
Sept. 1	Balance				18,700

Date	Explanation	Ref.	Debit	Credit	Balance

Date	Explanation	Ref.	Debit	Credit	Balance

(a), (c), and (e) (Continued)

Date	Explanation	Ref.	Debit	Credit	Balance

Date	Explanation	Ref.	Debit	Credit	Balance

Date	Explanation	Ref.	Debit	Credit	Balance

Date	Explanation	Ref.	Debit	Credit	Balance

Date	Explanation	Ref.	Debit	Credit	Balance

Date	Explanation	Ref.	Debit	Credit	Balance

Date	Explanation	Ref.	Debit	Credit	Balance

(b) and (e)

	General Journal			
Date	Account Titles and Explanation	Ref.	Debit	Credit

(d) and (f)

	(d) Unadjusted		(f) Adjusted	
	Debit	Credit	Debit	Credit

(g)

(b) (Continued)

Building

Date	Explanation	Ref.	Debit	Credit	Balance
Dec. 31	Balance				128,800

Accumulated Amortization - Building

Date	Explanation	Ref.	Debit	Credit	Balance
Dec. 31	Balance				45,600

Equipment

Date	Explanation	Ref.	Debit	Credit	Balance
Dec. 31	Balance				62,400

Accumulated Amortization - Equipment

Date	Explanation	Ref.	Debit	Credit	Balance
Dec. 31	Balance				17,770

Accounts Payable

Date	Explanation	Ref.	Debit	Credit	Balance
Dec. 31	Balance				12,300

Unearned Bowling Revenue

Date	Explanation	Ref.	Debit	Credit	Balance
Dec. 31	Balance				950

Interest Payable

Date	Explanation	Ref.	Debit	Credit	Balance
Dec. 31	Balance				2,600

Section

Date

(b) (Continued)

Mortgage Payable

Date	Explanation	Ref.	Debit	Credit	Balance
Dec. 31	Balance				94,780

Bolgos, Capital

Date	Explanation	Ref.	Debit	Credit	Balance
Dec. 31	Balance				115,000

Bowling Revenues

Date	Explanation	Ref.	Debit	Credit	Balance
Dec. 31	Balance				14,180

Insurance Expense

Date	Explanation	Ref.	Debit	Credit	Balance
Dec. 31	Balance				780

Amortization Expense

Date	Explanation	Ref.	Debit	Credit	Balance
Dec. 31	Balance				7,360

Interest Expense

Date	Explanation	Ref.	Debit	Credit	Balance
Dec. 31	Balance				2,600

E4-3 (Continued) (c)

	Debit	Credit

E4-4

General Journal

Date	Account Titles and Explanation	Ref.	Debit	Credit

(a)

(a), (b) and (c)   Cash

Date	Explanation	Ref.	Debit	Credit	Balance

Accounts Receivable

Date	Explanation	Ref.	Debit	Credit	Balance
Dec. 31	Balance				24,000

Interest Payable

Date	Explanation	Ref.	Debit	Credit	Balance
Dec. 31	Balance				0

Masterson, Capital

Date	Explanation	Ref.	Debit	Credit	Balance
Dec. 31	Balance				48,000

Commission Revenue

Date	Explanation	Ref.	Debit	Credit	Balance
Dec. 31	Balance				92,000

Interest Expense

Date	Explanation	Ref.	Debit	Credit	Balance
Dec. 31	Balance				7,750

(a) to (c)

General Journal

Date	Account Titles and Explanation	Ref.	Debit	Credit

(d)

(a)

(a) (Continued)

(b)

General Journal

Date	Account Titles and Explanation	Ref.	Debit	Credit

(c)

Cash

Date	Explanation	Ref.	Debit	Credit	Balance
Dec.31	Balance				6,600

Accounts Receivable

Date	Explanation	Ref.	Debit	Credit	Balance
Dec.31	Balance				13,500

Prepaid Insurance

Date	Explanation	Ref.	Debit	Credit	Balance
Dec.31	Balance				3,500

Supplies

Date	Explanation	Ref.	Debit	Credit	Balance
Dec.31	Balance				1,140

Land

Date	Explanation	Ref.	Debit	Credit	Balance
Dec.31	Balance				46,800

Building

Date	Explanation	Ref.	Debit	Credit	Balance
Dec.31	Balance				87,580

Accumulated Amortization - Building

Date	Explanation	Ref.	Debit	Credit	Balance
Dec.31	Balance				17,520

Name

Section

Date

(c) (Continued)

Equipment

Date	Explanation	Ref.	Debit	Credit	Balance
Dec.31	Balance				26,000

Accumulated Amortization - Equipment

Date	Explanation	Ref.	Debit	Credit	Balance
Dec.31	Balance				5,600

Accounts Payable

Date	Explanation	Ref.	Debit	Credit	Balance
Dec.31	Balance				13,220

Salaries Payable

Date	Explanation	Ref.	Debit	Credit	Balance
Dec.31	Balance				3,000

Interest Payable

Date	Explanation	Ref.	Debit	Credit	Balance
Dec.31	Balance				350

Unearned Revenue

Date	Explanation	Ref.	Debit	Credit	Balance
Dec.31	Balance				2,190

Notes Payable, Long-term

Date	Explanation	Ref.	Debit	Credit	Balance
Dec.31	Balance				63,900

(c) (Continued)

R. Ospina, Capital

Date	Explanation	Ref.	Debit	Credit	Balance
Dec.31	Balance				45,000

R. Ospina, Drawings

Date	Explanation	Ref.	Debit	Credit	Balance
Dec.31	Balance				12,000

Income Summary

Date	Explanation	Ref.	Debit	Credit	Balance

Salaries Expense

Date	Explanation	Ref.	Debit	Credit	Balance
Dec.31	Balance				32,100

Amortization Expense - Building

Date	Explanation	Ref.	Debit	Credit	Balance
Dec.31	Balance				3,500

Amortization Expense - Equipment

Date	Explanation	Ref.	Debit	Credit	Balance
Dec.31	Balance				2,800

(c) (Continued)

Utilities Expense

Date	Explanation	Ref.	Debit	Credit	Balance
Dec.31	Balance				2,175

Interest Expense

Date	Explanation	Ref.	Debit	Credit	Balance
Dec.31	Balance				5,115

Insurance Expense

Date	Explanation	Ref.	Debit	Credit	Balance
Dec.31	Balance				8,400

Supplies Expense

Date	Explanation	Ref.	Debit	Credit	Balance
Dec.31	Balance				2,170

(d)

	Debit	Credit

(a)

(a) (Continued)

(b)

General Journal

Date	Account Titles and Explanation	Ref.	Debit	Credit

(c)

Cash

Date	Explanation	Ref.	Debit	Credit	Balance
Dec.31	Balance				3,600

Temporary Investments

Date	Explanation	Ref.	Debit	Credit	Balance
Dec.31	Balance				3,000

Accounts Receivable

Date	Explanation	Ref.	Debit	Credit	Balance
Dec.31	Balance				5,400

Interest Receivable

Date	Explanation	Ref.	Debit	Credit	Balance
Dec.31	Balance				600

(c) (Continued)

Prepaid Insurance

Date	Explanation	Ref.	Debit	Credit	Balance
Dec.31	Balance				2,800

Supplies

Date	Explanation	Ref.	Debit	Credit	Balance
Dec.31	Balance				2,000

Notes Receivable

Date	Explanation	Ref.	Debit	Credit	Balance
Dec.31	Balance				7,500

Office Equipment

Date	Explanation	Ref.	Debit	Credit	Balance
Dec.31	Balance				34,000

Accumulated Amortization - Office Equipment

Date	Explanation	Ref.	Debit	Credit	Balance
Dec.31	Balance				8,000

Patent

Date	Explanation	Ref.	Debit	Credit	Balance
Dec.31	Balance				22,000

Note Payable

Date	Explanation	Ref.	Debit	Credit	Balance
Dec.31	Balance				18,000

(c) (Continued)

Accounts Payable

Date	Explanation	Ref.	Debit	Credit	Balance
Dec.31	Balance				6,000

Salaries Payable

Date	Explanation	Ref.	Debit	Credit	Balance
Dec.31	Balance				3,500

Interest Payable

Date	Explanation	Ref.	Debit	Credit	Balance
Dec.31	Balance				800

Unearned Revenue

Date	Explanation	Ref.	Debit	Credit	Balance
Dec.31	Balance				2,000

P. Cormier, Capital

Date	Explanation	Ref.	Debit	Credit	Balance
Dec.31	Balance				32,800

P. Cormier, Drawings

Date	Explanation	Ref.	Debit	Credit	Balance
Dec.31	Balance				10,000

Income Summary

Date	Explanation	Ref.	Debit	Credit	Balance

(c) (Continued)

Service Revenue

Date	Explanation	Ref.	Debit	Credit	Balance
Dec.31	Balance				88,000

Interest Revenue

Date	Explanation	Ref.	Debit	Credit	Balance
Dec.31	Balance				600

Amortization Expense

Date	Explanation	Ref.	Debit	Credit	Balance
Dec.31	Balance				8,000

Salaries Expense

Date	Explanation	Ref.	Debit	Credit	Balance
Dec.31	Balance				40,000

Rent Expense

Date	Explanation	Ref.	Debit	Credit	Balance
Dec.31	Balance				14,000

Insurance Expense

Date	Explanation	Ref.	Debit	Credit	Balance
Dec.31	Balance				5,000

Interest Expense

Date	Explanation	Ref.	Debit	Credit	Balance
Dec.31	Balance				1,800

(d)

	Debit	Credit

(a)

(1) Incorrect Entry

(2) Correct Entry

(3) Correcting Entry

(b)

	Debit	Credit

P 4-6A (a)	Income Statement			Balance Sheet		
Item	Revenue	Expenses	Net Income	Assets	Liabilities	Owner's Equity
1.	NE	NE	NE	U $ 500	U $ 500	NE
2.						
3.						
4.						
5.						
6.						
7.						
8.						
(b) Totals						

P 4-7A (a)		
Ratio	2002	2001
Working Capital		
Current Ratio		

(b)

(b)

(b) (Continued)

(c) and (d)

General Journal

Date	Account Titles and Explanation	Ref.	Debit	Credit

(a)

WATER WORLD PARK, Work Sheet, Year Ended September 30, 2005

Account Titles	Unadjusted Trial Balance		Adjustments		Adjusted Trial Balance		Income Statement		Balance Sheet	
	Dr.	Cr.	Dr.	Cr.	Dr.	Cr.	Dr.	Cr.	Dr.	Cr.
Cash	41,400									
Accounts receivable										
Supplies	18,600									
Prepaid insurance	31,900									
Land	80,000									
Building	500,000									
Accum. amortiz. - bldg.		125,000								
Equipment	120,000									
Accum. amortiz. - equip.		36,200								
Accounts payable		14,600								
Wages payable										
Interest payable										
Property taxes payable										
Unearned admission revenue		3,700								
Mortgage payable		350,000								
M. Berge, capital		159,700								
M. Berge, drawings	14,000									
Admission revenue		302,500								
Concession revenue		16,720								
Wages expense	105,000									
Repair expense	30,500									
Advertising expense	9,660									
Utilities expense	16,900									
Property tax expense	18,000									
Insurance expense										
Interest expense	22,460									
Amort. expense										
Supplies expense										
Totals	1,008,420	1,008,420								
Net income or loss										
Totals										

4-52

(b)

(c) and (d)

General Journal

Date	Account Titles and Explanation	Ref.	Debit	Credit

(e)

	Debit	Credit

*P4-11A

(a)		(n)
(b)		(o)
(c)		(p)
(d)		(q)
(e)		(r)
(f)		(s)
(g)		(t)
(h)		(u)
(i)		(v)
(j)		(w)
(k)		(x)
(l)		(y)
(m)		(z)

*P4-12A (a) 1.

General Journal

Date	Account Titles and Explanation	Ref.	Debit	Credit

(a) (Continued)

2.

Interest Receivable	
2,000	

Prepaid Insurance	
5,000	

Wages Payable	
	38,000

Unearned Sales Revenue	
	45,000

(b) 1. and 2.

General Journal

Date	Account Titles and Explanation	Ref.	Debit	Credit

(b) (Continued)

3.

Interest Receivable	
2,000	

Prepaid Insurance	
5,000	

Wages Payable	
	38,000

Unearned Sales Revenue	
	45,000

General Journal				
Date	Account Titles and Explanation	Ref.	Debit	Credit

P 4-1B (a)

Account	Normal Balance
Other Revenue	
Repair Service Expense	
Repair Service Revenue	
R. Laporte, Drawings	
R. Laporte, Capital	
Other Expense	
Income Summary	

(b)

General Journal

Date	Account Titles and Explanation	Ref.	Debit	Credit

(c)

Income Summary

(a)

General Journal

Date	Account Titles and Explanation	Ref.	Debit	Credit

(b)

	Debit	Credit

(c)

(c) (Continued)

(d)

General Journal

Date	Account Titles and Explanation	Ref.	Debit	Credit

(a)

(a) (Continued)

(b)

General Journal

Date	Account Titles and Explanation	Ref.	Debit	Credit

(c)

Cash

Date	Explanation	Ref.	Debit	Credit	Balance
Dec.31	Balance				10,200

Accounts Receivable

Date	Explanation	Ref.	Debit	Credit	Balance
Dec.31	Balance				7,500

Prepaid Insurance

Date	Explanation	Ref.	Debit	Credit	Balance
Dec.31	Balance				1,800

Supplies

Date	Explanation	Ref.	Debit	Credit	Balance
Dec.31	Balance				570

Land

Date	Explanation	Ref.	Debit	Credit	Balance
Dec.31	Balance				100,000

Building

Date	Explanation	Ref.	Debit	Credit	Balance
Dec.31	Balance				150,000

Accumulated Amortization - Building

Date	Explanation	Ref.	Debit	Credit	Balance
Dec.31	Balance				24,000

Name

Section

Date

(c) (Continued)

Equipment

Date	Explanation	Ref.	Debit	Credit	Balance
Dec.31	Balance				28,000

Accumulated Amortization - Equipment

Date	Explanation	Ref.	Debit	Credit	Balance
Dec.31	Balance				8,400

Accounts Payable

Date	Explanation	Ref.	Debit	Credit	Balance
Dec.31	Balance				12,000

Salaries Payable

Date	Explanation	Ref.	Debit	Credit	Balance
Dec.31	Balance				2,850

Interest Payable

Date	Explanation	Ref.	Debit	Credit	Balance
Dec.31	Balance				1,400

Unearned Revenue

Date	Explanation	Ref.	Debit	Credit	Balance
Dec.31	Balance				2,190

Mortgage Payable, long-term

Date	Explanation	Ref.	Debit	Credit	Balance
Dec.31	Balance				198,000

(c) (Continued)

A. Zazu, Capital

Date	Explanation	Ref.	Debit	Credit	Balance
Dec.31	Balance				54,500

A. Zazu, Drawings

Date	Explanation	Ref.	Debit	Credit	Balance
Dec.31	Balance				7,200

Income Summary

Date	Explanation	Ref.	Debit	Credit	Balance

Service Revenue

Date	Explanation	Ref.	Debit	Credit	Balance
Dec.31	Balance				77,500

Salaries Expense

Date	Explanation	Ref.	Debit	Credit	Balance
Dec.31	Balance				47,040

Amortization Expense - Building

Date	Explanation	Ref.	Debit	Credit	Balance
Dec.31	Balance				3,000

(c) (Continued)

Amortization Expense - Equipment

Date	Explanation	Ref.	Debit	Credit	Balance
Dec.31	Balance				2,800

Utilities Expense

Date	Explanation	Ref.	Debit	Credit	Balance
Dec.31	Balance				5,280

Interest Expense

Date	Explanation	Ref.	Debit	Credit	Balance
Dec.31	Balance				16,830

Insurance Expense

Date	Explanation	Ref.	Debit	Credit	Balance
Dec.31	Balance				1,200

Supplies Expense

Date	Explanation	Ref.	Debit	Credit	Balance
Dec.31	Balance				3,420

(d)

	Debit	Credit

(a)

(a) (Continued)

(b)

General Journal

Date	Account Titles and Explanation	Ref.	Debit	Credit

(c)

Cash

Date	Explanation	Ref.	Debit	Credit	Balance
Mar. 31	Balance				5,800

Temporary Investments

Date	Explanation	Ref.	Debit	Credit	Balance
Mar. 31	Balance				4,000

Accounts Receivable

Date	Explanation	Ref.	Debit	Credit	Balance
Mar. 31	Balance				6,200

Interest Receivable

Date	Explanation	Ref.	Debit	Credit	Balance
Mar. 31	Balance				800

(c) (Continued)

Prepaid Insurance

Date	Explanation	Ref.	Debit	Credit	Balance
Mar. 31	Balance				4,400

Supplies

Date	Explanation	Ref.	Debit	Credit	Balance
Mar. 31	Balance				2,300

Note Receivable

Date	Explanation	Ref.	Debit	Credit	Balance
Mar. 31	Balance				20,000

Computer Equipment

Date	Explanation	Ref.	Debit	Credit	Balance
Mar. 31	Balance				39,000

Accumulated Amortization - Computer Equipment

Date	Explanation	Ref.	Debit	Credit	Balance
Mar. 31	Balance				18,000

Patent

Date	Explanation	Ref.	Debit	Credit	Balance
Mar. 31	Balance				16,000

Note Payable

Date	Explanation	Ref.	Debit	Credit	Balance
Mar. 31	Balance				20,000

(c) (Continued)

Accounts Payable

Date	Explanation	Ref.	Debit	Credit	Balance
Mar. 31	Balance				8,000

Salaries Payable

Date	Explanation	Ref.	Debit	Credit	Balance
Mar. 31	Balance				2,600

Interest Payable

Date	Explanation	Ref.	Debit	Credit	Balance
Mar. 31	Balance				1,000

Unearned Revenue

Date	Explanation	Ref.	Debit	Credit	Balance
Mar. 31	Balance				1,200

N. Anderson, Capital

Date	Explanation	Ref.	Debit	Credit	Balance
Mar. 31	Balance				36,000

N. Anderson, Drawings

Date	Explanation	Ref.	Debit	Credit	Balance
Mar. 31	Balance				12,000

(c) (Continued)

Income Summary

Date	Explanation	Ref.	Debit	Credit	Balance

Service Revenue

Date	Explanation	Ref.	Debit	Credit	Balance
Mar. 31	Balance				79,800

Interest Revenue

Date	Explanation	Ref.	Debit	Credit	Balance
Mar. 31	Balance				600

Amortization Expense

Date	Explanation	Ref.	Debit	Credit	Balance
Mar. 31	Balance				6,000

Salaries Expense

Date	Explanation	Ref.	Debit	Credit	Balance
Mar. 31	Balance				39,000

Advertising Expense

Date	Explanation	Ref.	Debit	Credit	Balance
Mar. 31	Balance				12,000

Supplies Expense

Date	Explanation	Ref.	Debit	Credit	Balance
Mar. 31	Balance				3,700

(c) (Continued)

Insurance Expense

Date	Explanation	Ref.	Debit	Credit	Balance
Mar. 31	Balance				4,000

Interest Expense

Date	Explanation	Ref.	Debit	Credit	Balance
Mar. 31	Balance				2,000

(d)

	Debit	Credit

(a)

(1) Incorrect Entry	(2) Correct Entry	(3) Correcting Entry

(b)

	Debit	Credit

P4-6B (a)	Income Statement			Balance Sheet		
Item	Revenue	Expenses	Net Income	Assets	Liabilities	Owner's Equity
1.	NE	O $900	U $900	U $900	NE	U $900
2.						
3.						
4.						
5.						
6.						
7.						
8.						
9.						
(b) Totals						

P4-7B (a)	2002	2001	2000
Working Capital			
Current Ratio			

(b)

Edge Sports Repair Shop
Work Sheet
Year Ended September 30, 2005

Account Titles	Unadjusted Trial Balance		Adjustments		Adjusted Trial Balance		Income Statement		Balance Sheet	
	Dr.	Cr.	Dr.	Cr.	Dr.	Cr.	Dr.	Cr.	Dr.	Cr.
Cash	8,500									
Accounts receivable	1,450									
Prepaid insurance	4,140									
Supplies	3,780									
Land	55,000									
Building	95,000									
Accum. amortiz., building		11,875								
Equipment	36,000									
Accum. amortiz., equip.		9,000								
Accounts payable		4,300								
Unearned revenue		2,270								
Salaries payable										
Interest payable										
Mortgage payable		105,000								
L. Bachchan, capital		60,000								
L. Bachchan, drawings	93,525									
Service revenue		198,450								
Salaries expense	75,900									
Utilities expense	11,100									
Interest expense	6,500									
Insurance expense										
Supplies expense										
Amortization expense, bldg										
Amortization expense, equip.										
Totals	390,895	390,895								
Net income or loss										
Totals										

(a)

MASON P. I.
Work Sheet
Year Ended October 31, 2005

Account Titles	Unadjusted Trial Balance		Adjustments		Adjusted Trial Balance		Income Statement		Balance Sheet	
	Dr.	Cr.	Dr.	Cr.	Dr.	Cr.	Dr.	Cr.	Dr.	Cr.
Cash	9,618									
Accounts receivable	5,620									
Prepaid insurance	2,400									
Office supplies	1,050									
Vehicle	24,000									
Accum. amortiz., vehicle		8,000								
Office equipment	6,000									
Accum. amortiz., office equipment		2,400								
Notes payable		10,000								
Accounts payable		2,350								
Salaries payable										
Unearned service revenue		3,000								
Interest payable										
A. Mason, capital		20,000								
A. Mason, drawings	29,000									
Service revenue		54,480								
Salaries expense	10,800									
Interest expense	917									
Rent expense	4,800									
Telephone expense	825									
Gas and oil expense	5,200									
Amortization expense										
Insurance expense										
Supplies expense										
Totals	100,230	100,230								
Net income or loss										
Totals										

4-86

(b)

(b) (Continued)

(c) and (d)

General Journal

Date	Account Titles and Explanation	Ref.	Debit	Credit

(a)

KUMAR MANAGEMENT SERVICES, Work Sheet, Year Ended December 31, 2005

Account Titles	Unadjusted Trial Balance		Adjustments		Adjusted Trial Balance		Income Statement		Balance Sheet	
	Dr.	Cr.	Dr.	Cr.	Dr.	Cr.	Dr.	Cr.	Dr.	Cr.
Cash	14,310									
Accounts receivable	23,600									
Supplies	3,150									
Prepaid insurance	3,100									
Land	56,000									
Building	106,000									
Accum. amortiz. - bldg.		22,500								
Equipment	49,000									
Accum. amortiz. - equip.		16,000								
Accounts payable		10,400								
Salaries payable										
Interest payable										
Property taxes payable										
Unearned rent revenue		5,000								
Mortgage payable		100,000								
N. Kumar, capital		113,150								
N. Kumar, drawings	28,500									
Service revenue		75,600								
Rent revenue		24,000								
Salaries expense	30,000									
Repairs expense	8,675									
Advertising expense	17,000									
Utilities expense	15,800									
Property tax expense	5,265									
Insurance expense										
Interest expense	6,250									
Amortiz. exp., bldg										
Amortiz. exp., equip										
Supplies expense										
Totals	366,650	366,650								
Net income or loss										
Totals										

4-90

(b)

(c) and (d)

General Journal

Date	Account Titles and Explanation	Ref.	Debit	Credit

(e)

	Debit	Credit

*P4-11B	
(a)	(n)
(b)	(o)
(c)	(p)
(d)	(q)
(e)	(r)
(f)	(s)
(g)	(t)
(h)	(u)
(i)	(v)
(j)	(w)
(k)	(x)
(l)	(y)
(m)	(z)

*P4-12B (a) 1.

General Journal

Date	Account Titles and Explanation	Ref.	Debit	Credit

(a) (Continued)

2.

Rent Receivable	
3,000	

Prepaid Insurance	
4,800	

Property Taxes Payable	
	3,250

Unearned Service Revenue	
	35,000

(b) 1. and 2.

General Journal

Date	Account Titles and Explanation	Ref.	Debit	Credit

(b) (Continued)

3.

Rent Receivable	
3,000	

Prepaid Insurance	
4,800	

Property Taxes Payable	
	3,250

Unearned Service Revenue	
	35,000

General Journal				
Date	Account Titles and Explanation	Ref.	Debit	Credit

(a), (c), and (f) (Continued)

Baking Equipment

Date	Explanation	Ref.	Debit	Credit	Balance
Nov. 30	Balance				1,200

Accumulated Amortization - Baking Equipment

Date	Explanation	Ref.	Debit	Credit	Balance
Nov. 30	Balance				20

Website

Date	Explanation	Ref.	Debit	Credit	Balance
Nov. 30	Balance				600

Accumulated Amortization--Website

Date	Explanation	Ref.	Debit	Credit	Balance

Accounts Payable

Date	Explanation	Ref.	Debit	Credit	Balance
Nov. 30	Balance				650

Salaries Payable

Date	Explanation	Ref.	Debit	Credit	Balance

Interest Payable

Date	Explanation	Ref.	Debit	Credit	Balance
Nov. 30	Balance				5

(a), (c), and (f) (Continued)

Unearned Revenue

Date	Explanation	Ref.	Debit	Credit	Balance
Nov. 30	Balance				25

Note Payable

Date	Explanation	Ref.	Debit	Credit	Balance
Nov. 30	Balance				2,000

N. Koebel, Capital

Date	Explanation	Ref.	Debit	Credit	Balance
Nov. 30	Balance				800

N. Koebel, Drawings

Date	Explanation	Ref.	Debit	Credit	Balance

Income Summary

Date	Explanation	Ref.	Debit	Credit	Balance

Teaching Revenue

Date	Explanation	Ref.	Debit	Credit	Balance
Nov. 30	Balance				350

(a), (c), and (f) (Continued)

Salaries Expense

Date	Explanation	Ref.	Debit	Credit	Balance

Telephone Expense

Date	Explanation	Ref.	Debit	Credit	Balance
Nov. 30	Balance				50

Advertising Supplies Expense

Date	Explanation	Ref.	Debit	Credit	Balance
Nov. 30	Balance				20

Banking Supplies Expense

Date	Explanation	Ref.	Debit	Credit	Balance
Nov. 30	Balance				25

Amortization Expense, Baking Equipment

Date	Explanation	Ref.	Debit	Credit	Balance
Nov. 30	Balance				20

Amortization Expense, Website

Date	Explanation	Ref.	Debit	Credit	Balance

Insurance Expense

Date	Explanation	Ref.	Debit	Credit	Balance

(a), (c), and (f) (Continued)

Interest Expense

Date	Explanation	Ref.	Debit	Credit	Balance
Nov. 30	Balance				5

Date	Explanation	Ref.	Debit	Credit	Balance

Date	Explanation	Ref.	Debit	Credit	Balance

Date	Explanation	Ref.	Debit	Credit	Balance

Date	Explanation	Ref.	Debit	Credit	Balance

Date	Explanation	Ref.	Debit	Credit	Balance

Date	Explanation	Ref.	Debit	Credit	Balance

(g)

	Debit	Credit

(a)

General Journal

Date	Account Titles and Explanation	Ref.	Debit	Credit

(b)

	Debit	Credit

(c)

General Journal

Date	Account Titles and Explanation	Ref.	Debit	Credit

(d)

	Debit	Credit

Section _____

Date _____

(a), (c) and (f)

Cash

Date	Explanation	Ref.	Debit	Credit	Balance

Accounts Receivable

Date	Explanation	Ref.	Debit	Credit	Balance

Cleaning Supplies

Date	Explanation	Ref.	Debit	Credit	Balance

Prepaid Insurance

Date	Explanation	Ref.	Debit	Credit	Balance

Equipment

Date	Explanation	Ref.	Debit	Credit	Balance

(a), (c) and (f) (Continued)

Accumulated Amortization - Equipment

Date	Explanation	Ref.	Debit	Credit	Balance

Accounts Payable

Date	Explanation	Ref.	Debit	Credit	Balance

Salaries Payable

Date	Explanation	Ref.	Debit	Credit	Balance

Lee Chan, Capital

Date	Explanation	Ref.	Debit	Credit	Balance

Income Summary

Date	Explanation	Ref.	Debit	Credit	Balance

Lee Chan, Drawings

Date	Explanation	Ref.	Debit	Credit	Balance

Section

Date

(a), (c) and (f) (Continued)   Cleaning Revenue

Date	Explanation	Ref.	Debit	Credit	Balance

Gas & Oil Expense

Date	Explanation	Ref.	Debit	Credit	Balance

Cleaning Supplies Expense

Date	Explanation	Ref.	Debit	Credit	Balance

Amortization Expense

Date	Explanation	Ref.	Debit	Credit	Balance

Insurance Expense

Date	Explanation	Ref.	Debit	Credit	Balance

Salaries Expense

Date	Explanation	Ref.	Debit	Credit	Balance

Rent Expense

Date	Explanation	Ref.	Debit	Credit	Balance

(e)

(e) (Continued)

(f)

General Journal

Date	Account Titles and Explanation	Ref.	Debit	Credit

(g)

	Debit	Credit

BE5-1

BE5-2

BE5-3 and 5-4

General Journal

Date	Account Titles and Explanation	Ref.	Debit	Credit

BE5-5

General Journal

Date	Account Titles and Explanation	Ref.	Debit	Credit

Quantity:

Cost per package:

Total cost:

BE5-6 and 5-7

General Journal

Date	Account Titles and Explanation	Ref.	Debit	Credit

BE5-8

Item	Section	
	(1) Multiple-Step Income Statement	(2) Single-Step Income Statement
(a) Gain on sale of equipment		
(b) Interest expense		
(c) Cost of goods sold		
(d) Rent revenue		
(e) Amortization expense		

BE5-9

BE5-10

*BE5-11

General Journal

Date	Account Titles and Explanation	Ref.	Debit	Credit

*BE5-12

General Journal

Date	Account Titles and Explanation	Ref.	Debit	Credit

*BE5-13

*BE5-14

*BE5-15

General Journal

Date	Account Titles and Explanation	Ref.	Debit	Credit

*BE5-16

General Journal

Date	Account Titles and Explanation	Ref.	Debit	Credit

General Journal				
Date	Account Titles and Explanation	Ref.	Debit	Credit

Section

Date

(a)

General Journal

Date	Account Titles and Explanation	Ref.	Debit	Credit

(b)

Merchandise Inventory

Date	Explanation	Ref.	Debit	Credit	Balance

Cost of Goods Sold

Date	Explanation	Ref.	Debit	Credit	Balance

General Journal				
Date	Account Titles and Explanation	Ref.	Debit	Credit

(a)

(b)

Account	Statement	Classification
Accounts Payable	Balance Sheet	Current Liabilities
Accounts Receivable		
Accumulated Amortization - Office Building		
Accumulated Amortization - Store Equipment		
Advertising Expense		
Amortization Expense		
B. Swirsky, Capital		
B. Swirsky, Drawings		
Cash		
Freight Out		
Insurance Expense		
Interest Expense		
Interest Payable		
Land		
Merchandise Inventory		
Mortgage Payable		
Office Building		
Prepaid Insurance		
Property Tax Payable		
Salaries Expense		
Salaries Payable		
Sales Returns and Allowances		
Store Equipment		
Unearned Sales Revenue		
Utilities Expense		

E5-9

*E5-10 (a)

General Journal

Date	Account Titles and Explanation	Ref.	Debit	Credit

*E5-10 (b) and (c)	

*E5-11	

(a)

(b)

General Journal

Date	Account Titles and Explanation	Ref.	Debit	Credit

	General Journal			
Date	Account Titles and Explanation	Ref.	Debit	Credit

General Journal				
Date	Account Titles and Explanation	Ref.	Debit	Credit

General Journal				
Date	Account Titles and Explanation	Ref.	Debit	Credit

(a)

General Journal

Date	Account Titles and Explanation	Ref.	Debit	Credit

(b)

Cash

Date	Explanation	Ref.	Debit	Credit	Balance
April 1	Balance				9,000

Accounts Receivable

Date	Explanation	Ref.	Debit	Credit	Balance

Merchandise Inventory

Date	Explanation	Ref.	Debit	Credit	Balance

(b) (Continued)

Accounts Payable

Date	Explanation	Ref.	Debit	Credit	Balance

M. Nisson, Capital

Date	Explanation	Ref.	Debit	Credit	Balance
April 1	Balance				9,000

Sales

Date	Explanation	Ref.	Debit	Credit	Balance

Sales Returns and Allowances

Date	Explanation	Ref.	Debit	Credit	Balance

Cost of Goods Sold

Date	Explanation	Ref.	Debit	Credit	Balance

Freight Out

Date	Explanation	Ref.	Debit	Credit	Balance

(c)

(d)

(a)

General Journal

Date	Account Titles and Explanation	Ref.	Debit	Credit

(b)

(b) (Continued)

(c)

General Journal

Date	Account Titles and Explanation	Ref.	Debit	Credit

(a)

General Journal

Date	Account Titles and Explanation	Ref.	Debit	Credit

(b)

(b) (Continued)

(c)

General Journal

Date	Account Titles and Explanation	Ref.	Debit	Credit

(a)

General Journal

Date	Account Titles and Explanation	Ref.	Debit	Credit

(b)

	Debit	Credit

(c)

(c) (Continued)

(d)

General Journal

Date	Account Titles and Explanation	Ref.	Debit	Credit

(a)

(a) (Continued)

P5-6A (b)

General Journal

Date	Account Titles and Explanation	Ref.	Debit	Credit

(c)

P5-7A (a)

	2002	2001
Gross profit margin		
Profit margin		
Current ratio		

(b)

	General Journal			
Date	Account Titles and Explanation	Ref.	Debit	Credit

(a)

General Journal

Date	Account Titles and Explanation	Ref.	Debit	Credit

(b)

Cash

Date	Explanation	Ref.	Debit	Credit	Balance
April 1	Balance				2,500

Accounts Receivable

Date	Explanation	Ref.	Debit	Credit	Balance

Merchandise Inventory

Date	Explanation	Ref.	Debit	Credit	Balance
April 1	Balance				3,500

Supplies

Date	Explanation	Ref.	Debit	Credit	Balance

Accounts Payable

Date	Explanation	Ref.	Debit	Credit	Balance

(b) (Continued)

J. Kane, Capital

Date	Explanation	Ref.	Debit	Credit	Balance
April 1	Balance				6,000

Sales

Date	Explanation	Ref.	Debit	Credit	Balance

Sales Returns and Allowances

Date	Explanation	Ref.	Debit	Credit	Balance

Purchases

Date	Explanation	Ref.	Debit	Credit	Balance

Purchase Returns and Allowances

Date	Explanation	Ref.	Debit	Credit	Balance

Freight In

Date	Explanation	Ref.	Debit	Credit	Balance

(c)

	Debit	Credit

(d)

(a)

(b)

General Journal

Date	Account Titles and Explanation	Ref.	Debit	Credit

(c)

B. Hachey, Capital

Date	Explanation	Ref.	Debit	Credit	Balance
Dec. 1	Balance				155,750

(a)

General Journal

Date	Account Titles and Explanation	Ref.	Debit	Credit

(b)

Cash

Date	Explanation	Ref.	Debit	Credit	Balance
Sept.1	Balance				70,000

Accounts Receivable

Date	Explanation	Ref.	Debit	Credit	Balance

Merchandise Inventory

Date	Explanation	Ref.	Debit	Credit	Balance

Accounts Payable

Date	Explanation	Ref.	Debit	Credit	Balance

(b) (Continued)

C. Norlan, Capital

Date	Explanation	Ref.	Debit	Credit	Balance
Sept.1	Balance				70,000

Sales

Date	Explanation	Ref.	Debit	Credit	Balance

Sales Returns and Allowances

Date	Explanation	Ref.	Debit	Credit	Balance

Sales Discounts

Date	Explanation	Ref.	Debit	Credit	Balance

Cost of Goods Sold

Date	Explanation	Ref.	Debit	Credit	Balance

(c)

(a)

General Journal

Date	Account Titles and Explanation	Ref.	Debit	Credit

(b)

Cash

Date	Explanation	Ref.	Debit	Credit	Balance
Sept.1	Balance				70,000

Accounts Receivable

Date	Explanation	Ref.	Debit	Credit	Balance

Accounts Payable

Date	Explanation	Ref.	Debit	Credit	Balance

C. Norlan, Capital

Date	Explanation	Ref.	Debit	Credit	Balance
Sept.1	Balance				70,000

Sales

Date	Explanation	Ref.	Debit	Credit	Balance

(b) (Continued)

Sales Returns and Allowances

Date	Explanation	Ref.	Debit	Credit	Balance

Sales Discounts

Date	Explanation	Ref.	Debit	Credit	Balance

Purchases

Date	Explanation	Ref.	Debit	Credit	Balance

Purchase Returns and Allowances

Date	Explanation	Ref.	Debit	Credit	Balance

Purchase Discounts

Date	Explanation	Ref.	Debit	Credit	Balance

Freight In

Date	Explanation	Ref.	Debit	Credit	Balance

(c)

(c)

	General Journal			
Date	Account Titles and Explanation	Ref.	Debit	Credit

(a)

General Journal

Date	Account Titles and Explanation	Ref.	Debit	Credit

(a) (Continued)

General Journal

Date	Account Titles and Explanation	Ref.	Debit	Credit

(b)

Cash

Date	Explanation	Ref.	Debit	Credit	Balance
May 1	Balance				5,000

Accounts Receivable

Date	Explanation	Ref.	Debit	Credit	Balance

Merchandise Inventory

Date	Explanation	Ref.	Debit	Credit	Balance

(b) (Continued)

Supplies

Date	Explanation	Ref.	Debit	Credit	Balance

Accounts Payable

Date	Explanation	Ref.	Debit	Credit	Balance

B. Copple, Capital

Date	Explanation	Ref.	Debit	Credit	Balance
May 1	Balance				5,000

Sales

Date	Explanation	Ref.	Debit	Credit	Balance

Sales Returns and Allowances

Date	Explanation	Ref.	Debit	Credit	Balance

Cost of Goods Sold

Date	Explanation	Ref.	Debit	Credit	Balance

(b) (Continued)

Freight Out

Date		Ref.	Debit	Credit	Balance

(c)

(d)

(a)

General Journal

Date	Account Titles and Explanation	Ref.	Debit	Credit

(b)

(b) (Continued)

(c)

General Journal

Date	Account Titles and Explanation	Ref.	Debit	Credit

(a)

General Journal

Date	Account Titles and Explanation	Ref.	Debit	Credit

(b)

(b) (Continued)

(c)

General Journal

Date	Account Titles and Explanation	Ref.	Debit	Credit

(a)

General Journal

Date	Account Titles and Explanation	Ref.	Debit	Credit

(b)

	Debit	Credit

(c)

(c) (Continued)

(d)

General Journal

Date	Account Titles and Explanation	Ref.	Debit	Credit

(a)

(a) (Continued)

P5-6B (b)

General Journal

Date	Account Titles and Explanation	Ref.	Debit	Credit

(c)

P5-7B (a)

	2002	2001
Gross profit margin		
Profit margin		
Current ratio		

(b)

	General Journal			
Date	Account Titles and Explanation	Ref.	Debit	Credit

(a)

General Journal

Date	Account Titles and Explanation	Ref.	Debit	Credit

(b)

Cash

Date	Explanation	Ref.	Debit	Credit	Balance
April 1	Balance				2,500

Accounts Receivable

Date	Explanation	Ref.	Debit	Credit	Balance

Merchandise Inventory

Date	Explanation	Ref.	Debit	Credit	Balance
April 1	Balance				1,700

Store Supplies

Date	Explanation	Ref.	Debit	Credit	Balance

Store Equipment

Date	Explanation	Ref.	Debit	Credit	Balance

(b) (Continued)

Accounts Payable

Date	Explanation	Ref.	Debit	Credit	Balance

J. Noya, Capital

Date	Explanation	Ref.	Debit	Credit	Balance
April 1	Balance				4,200

Sales

Date	Explanation	Ref.	Debit	Credit	Balance

Sales Returns and Allowances

Date	Explanation	Ref.	Debit	Credit	Balance

Purchases

Date	Explanation	Ref.	Debit	Credit	Balance

Purchase Returns and Allowances

Date	Explanation	Ref.	Debit	Credit	Balance

(b) (Continued)

Freight In

Date	Explanation	Ref.	Debit	Credit	Balance

(c)

	Debit	Credit

(d)

(a)

(b)

General Journal

Date	Account Titles and Explanation	Ref.	Debit	Credit

(c)

Merchandise Inventory

Date	Explanation	Ref.	Debit	Credit	Balance
Jan. 1	Balance				40,500

H. Tse, Capital

Date	Explanation	Ref.	Debit	Credit	Balance
Jan. 1	Balance				176,400

(a)

General Journal

Date	Account Titles and Explanation	Ref.	Debit	Credit

(b)

Cash

Date	Explanation	Ref.	Debit	Credit	Balance
Oct. 1	Balance				90,000

Accounts Receivable

Date	Explanation	Ref.	Debit	Credit	Balance

Merchandise Inventory

Date	Explanation	Ref.	Debit	Credit	Balance

Accounts Payable

Date	Explanation	Ref.	Debit	Credit	Balance

(b) (Continued)

D. Leeland, Capital

Date	Explanation	Ref.	Debit	Credit	Balance
Oct. 1	Balance				90,000

Sales

Date	Explanation	Ref.	Debit	Credit	Balance

Sales Returns and Allowances

Date	Explanation	Ref.	Debit	Credit	Balance

Sales Discounts

Date	Explanation	Ref.	Debit	Credit	Balance

Cost of Goods Sold

Date	Explanation	Ref.	Debit	Credit	Balance

Freight Out

Date	Explanation	Ref.	Debit	Credit	Balance

(c)

(a)

General Journal

Date	Account Titles and Explanation	Ref.	Debit	Credit

(b)

Cash

Date	Explanation	Ref.	Debit	Credit	Balance
Oct. 1	Balance				90,000

Accounts Receivable

Date	Explanation	Ref.	Debit	Credit	Balance

Accounts Payable

Date	Explanation	Ref.	Debit	Credit	Balance

D. Leeland, Capital

Date	Explanation	Ref.	Debit	Credit	Balance
Oct. 1	Balance				90,000

Sales

Date	Explanation	Ref.	Debit	Credit	Balance

(b) (Continued)

Sales Returns and Allowances

Date	Explanation	Ref.	Debit	Credit	Balance

Sales Discounts

Date	Explanation	Ref.	Debit	Credit	Balance

Purchases

Date	Explanation	Ref.	Debit	Credit	Balance

Purchase Returns and Allowances

Date	Explanation	Ref.	Debit	Credit	Balance

Purchase Discounts

Date	Explanation	Ref.	Debit	Credit	Balance

Freight In

Date	Explanation	Ref.	Debit	Credit	Balance

Freight Out

Date	Explanation	Ref.	Debit	Credit	Balance

(c)

(a)

(b)

General Journal

Date	Account Titles and Explanation	Ref.	Debit	Credit

(b) (Continued)

General Journal

Date	Account Titles and Explanation	Ref.	Debit	Credit

(b) and (d)

Cash

Date	Explanation	Ref.	Debit	Credit	Balance
Jan. 1	Balance				1,130

Accounts Receivable

Date	Explanation	Ref.	Debit	Credit	Balance
Jan. 1	Balance				875

Merchandise Inventory

Date	Explanation	Ref.	Debit	Credit	Balance

Advertising Supplies

Date	Explanation	Ref.	Debit	Credit	Balance
Jan. 1	Balance				50

(b) and (d) (Continued)

Baking Supplies

Date	Explanation	Ref.	Debit	Credit	Balance
Jan. 1	Balance				350

Prepaid Insurance

Date	Explanation	Ref.	Debit	Credit	Balance
Jan. 1	Balance				1,100

Baking Equipment

Date	Explanation	Ref.	Debit	Credit	Balance
Jan. 1	Balance				1,200

Accumulated Amortization, Baking Equipment

Date	Explanation	Ref.	Debit	Credit	Balance
Jan. 1	Balance				40

Website

Date	Explanation	Ref.	Debit	Credit	Balance
Jan. 1	Balance				600

Accumulated Amortization, Website

Date	Explanation	Ref.	Debit	Credit	Balance
Jan. 1	Balance				25

(b) and (d) (Continued)

Accounts Payable

Date	Explanation	Ref.	Debit	Credit	Balance
Jan. 1	Balance				75

Salaries Payable

Date	Explanation	Ref.	Debit	Credit	Balance
Jan. 1	Balance				56

Interest Payable

Date	Explanation	Ref.	Debit	Credit	Balance
Jan. 1	Balance				15

Unearned Revenue

Date	Explanation	Ref.	Debit	Credit	Balance
Jan. 1	Balance				300

Notes Payable

Date	Explanation	Ref.	Debit	Credit	Balance
Jan. 1	Balance				2,000

N. Koebel, Capital

Date	Explanation	Ref.	Debit	Credit	Balance
Jan. 1	Balance				2,794

(b) and (d) (Continued)

N. Koebel, Drawings

Date	Explanation	Ref.	Debit	Credit	Balance

Sales Revenue

Date	Explanation	Ref.	Debit	Credit	Balance

Cost of Goods Sold

Date	Explanation	Ref.	Debit	Credit	Balance

Salaries Expense

Date	Explanation	Ref.	Debit	Credit	Balance

Telephone Expense

Date	Explanation	Ref.	Debit	Credit	Balance

Amortization Expense, Baking Equipment

Date	Explanation	Ref.	Debit	Credit	Balance

Amortization Expense, Website

Date	Explanation	Ref.	Debit	Credit	Balance

(b) and (d) (Continued)

Insurance Expense

Date	Explanation	Ref.	Debit	Credit	Balance

Freight Out

Date	Explanation	Ref.	Debit	Credit	Balance

Interest Expense

Date	Explanation	Ref.	Debit	Credit	Balance

(c)

	Debit	Credit

(d)

General Journal

Date	Account Titles and Explanation	Ref.	Debit	Credit

Section _____

Date _____

(e)

	Debit	Credit

(f)

(g)

(a), (b), (d) and (g)

Cash

Date	Explanation	Ref.	Debit	Credit	Balance
Aug. 1	Balance				15,740

Accounts Receivable

Date	Explanation	Ref.	Debit	Credit	Balance
Aug. 1	Balance				2,975

Merchandise Inventory

Date	Explanation	Ref.	Debit	Credit	Balance
Aug. 1	Balance				112,700

(a), (b), (d) and (g) (Continued)

Store Supplies

Date	Explanation	Ref.	Debit	Credit	Balance
Aug. 1	Balance				2,660

Prepaid Insurance

Date	Explanation	Ref.	Debit	Credit	Balance
Aug. 1	Balance				4,140

Store Equipment

Date	Explanation	Ref.	Debit	Credit	Balance
Aug. 1	Balance				53,800

Accumulated Amortization - Store Equipment

Date	Explanation	Ref.	Debit	Credit	Balance
Aug. 1	Balance				13,450

Accounts Payable

Date	Explanation	Ref.	Debit	Credit	Balance
Aug. 1	Balance				22,120

Unearned Sales Revenue

Date	Explanation	Ref.	Debit	Credit	Balance
Aug. 1	Balance				4,820

(a), (b), (d) and (g) (Continued)

Notes Payable

Date	Explanation	Ref.	Debit	Credit	Balance
Aug. 1	Balance				36,000

Interest Payable

Date	Explanation	Ref.	Debit	Credit	Balance
Aug. 1	Balance				0

Salaries Payable

Date	Explanation	Ref.	Debit	Credit	Balance
Aug. 1	Balance				0

Andrew John, Capital

Date	Explanation	Ref.	Debit	Credit	Balance
Aug. 1	Balance				47,250

Andrew John, Drawings

Date	Explanation	Ref.	Debit	Credit	Balance
Aug. 1	Balance				42,000

Income Summary

Date	Explanation	Ref.	Debit	Credit	Balance

(a), (b), (d) and (g) (Continued)

Sales Revenue

Date	Explanation	Ref.	Debit	Credit	Balance
Aug. 1	Balance				761,300

Sales Returns and Allowances

Date	Sales Returns and Allowance	Ref.	Debit	Credit	Balance
Aug. 1	Balance				11,420

Cost of Goods Sold

Date	Explanation	Ref.	Debit	Credit	Balance
Aug. 1	Balance				517,680

Salaries Expense

Date	Explanation	Ref.	Debit	Credit	Balance
Aug. 1	Balance				92,900

(a), (b), (d) and (g) (Continued)

Advertising Expense

Date	Explanation	Ref.	Debit	Credit	Balance
Aug. 1	Balance				9,625

Rent Expense

Date	Explanation	Ref.	Debit	Credit	Balance
Aug. 1	Balance				17,050

Interest Expense

Date	Sales Returns and Allowance	Ref.	Debit	Credit	Balance
Aug. 1	Balance				2,250

Insurance Expense

Date	Explanation	Ref.	Debit	Credit	Balance
Aug. 1	Balance				0

Stores Supplies Expense

Date	Explanation	Ref.	Debit	Credit	Balance
Aug. 1	Balance				0

Amortization Expense

Date	Explanation	Ref.	Debit	Credit	Balance
Aug. 1	Balance				0

(b)

General Journal

Date	Account Titles and Explanation	Ref.	Debit	Credit

(b) (Continued)

General Journal

Date	Account Titles and Explanation	Ref.	Debit	Credit

Name

Section

Date

(c)

	Debit	Credit

(d)

General Journal

Date	Account Titles and Explanation	Ref.	Debit	Credit

(e)

	Debit	Credit

(f)

(f) (Continued)

(g)

General Journal

Date	Account Titles and Explanation	Ref.	Debit	Credit

(h)

	Debit	Credit

BE6-1

BE6-2

(a) FIFO

	Cost of Goods Sold				Ending Inventory		
Date	Units	Unit Cost	Total Cost	Date	Units	Unit Cost	Total Cost

(b) Average Cost

	Cost of Goods Sold Available for Sale					Wt. Ave.	
Date	Units	Unit Cost	Total Cost		Units	Unit Cost	Total Cost
				CGS			
				EI			

(c) LIFO

	Cost of Goods Sold				Ending Inventory		
Date	Units	Unit Cost	Total Cost	Date	Units	Unit Cost	Total Cost

(d) Specific Identification

	Cost of Goods Sold				Ending Inventory		
Date	Units	Unit Cost	Total Cost	Date	Units	Unit Cost	Total Cost

BE6-4

(a) FIFO

	Cost of Goods Sold				Ending Inventory		
Date	Units	Unit Cost	Total Cost	Date	Units	Unit Cost	Total Cost

(b) Average Cost

	Cost of Goods Sold Available for Sale					Wt. Ave.	
Date	Units	Unit Cost	Total Cost		Units	Unit Cost	Total Cost
				CGS			
				EI			

(c) LIFO

	Cost of Goods Sold				Ending Inventory		
Date	Units	Unit Cost	Total Cost	Date	Units	Unit Cost	Total Cost

BE6-5

BE6-6

BE6-7

BE6-8

	Assets	=	Liabilities	+	Owner's Equity
2004					
2005					

BE6-9

Inventory Item	Cost	Market	LCM	
Cameras				
DVD players				
VCRs				

BE6-10

BE6-11

(a) FIFO

Date	Purchases			Cost of Goods Sold			Balance		
	Units	Cost	Total	Units	Cost	Total	Units	Cost	Total

(b) Average Cost

Date	Purchases			Cost of Goods Sold			Balance		
	Units	Cost	Total	Units	Cost	Total	Units	Cost	Total

(c) LIFO

Date	Purchases			Cost of Goods Sold			Balance		
	Units	Cost	Total	Units	Cost	Total	Units	Cost	Total

(a) FIFO

Sequence	Purchases			Cost of Goods Sold			Balance		
	Units	Cost	Total	Units	Cost	Total	Units	Cost	Total

(b) Average Cost

Sequence	Purchases			Cost of Goods Sold			Balance		
	Units	Cost	Total	Units	Cost	Total	Units	Cost	Total

General Journal				
Date	Account Titles and Explanation	Ref.	Debit	Credit

*BE6-15

*BE6-16	At Cost	At Retail

E6-1

E6-2

E6-3

E6-4 FIFO

	Cost of Goods Sold				Ending Inventory		
Date	Units	Unit Cost	Total Cost	Date	Units	Unit Cost	Total Cost

E6-4 Average Cost

	Cost of Goods Sold Available for Sale				Units	Wt. Ave. Unit Cost	Total Cost
Date	Units	Unit Cost	Total Cost				
				CGS			
				EI			

E6-5 (a) (1) FIFO

	Cost of Goods Sold				Ending Inventory		
Date	Units	Unit Cost	Total Cost	Date	Units	Unit Cost	Total Cost

(a) (2) Average Cost

	Cost of Goods Sold Available for Sale				Units	Wt. Ave. Unit Cost	Total Cost
Date	Units	Unit Cost	Total Cost				
				CGS			
				EI			

E6-5 (b) to (d)

E6-6 (a) LIFO

Cost of Goods Sold				Ending Inventory			
Date	Units	Unit Cost	Total Cost	Date	Units	Unit Cost	Total Cost

(b)

E6-7 (a)

SELES HARDWARE
Income Statement (Partial)

	2004	2005
Beginning inventory		
Cost of goods purchased		
Cost of goods available for sale		
Ending inventory		
Cost of goods sold		

(b)

E6-8 (a)

	2004	2005

(b) to (d)

E6-9	2003	2002
Inventory turnover		
Days sales in inventory		
Gross profit margin		

E6-10			
(a) and (b)	Cost	Market	LCM
Cameras			
Minolta			
Canon			
Light meters			
Vivitar			
Kodak			

(c)

(a) (1) FIFO

Date	Purchases			Cost of Goods Sold			Balance		
	Units	Cost	Total	Units	Cost	Total	Units	Cost	Total

(a) (2) Average Cost

Date	Purchases			Cost of Goods Sold			Balance		
	Units	Cost	Total	Units	Cost	Total	Units	Cost	Total

(a) (Continued)

(a) (3) LIFO

Date	Purchases			Cost of Goods Sold			Balance		
	Units	Cost	Total	Units	Cost	Total	Units	Cost	Total

(b) and (c)

(a) FIFO

Date	Purchases			Cost of Goods Sold			Balance		
	Units	Cost	Total	Units	Cost	Total	Units	Cost	Total

(a) Average Cost

Date	Purchases			Cost of Goods Sold			Balance		
	Units	Cost	Total	Units	Cost	Total	Units	Cost	Total

(b) FIFO

	Cost of Goods Sold				Ending Inventory		
Date	Units	Unit Cost	Total Cost	Date	Units	Unit Cost	Total Cost

(b) Average Cost

	Cost of Goods Sold Available for Sale					Wt. Ave. Unit	
Date	Units	Unit Cost	Total Cost		Units	Cost	Total Cost
				CGS			
				EI			

			(1) FIFO		(2) Average	
Date	Account Titles and Explanation	Ref.	Dr.	Cr.	Dr.	Cr.

General Journal

*E6-14

*E6-15	Women's Department		Men's Department	
	Cost	Retail	Cost	Retail

(a)

(b)

	Running Shoes		Running Clothes	
	Cost	Retail	Cost	Retail

(c)

P6-1A

P6-2A (a)

(b) (1) FIFO

(1) Cost of Goods Sold				(2) Ending Inventory			
Date	Units	Unit Cost	Total Cost	Date	Units	Unit Cost	Total Cost

(b) (Continued)

(b) (2) Average Cost

Cost of Goods Sold Available for Sale					Units	Wt. Ave. Unit Cost	Total Cost
Date	Units	Unit Cost	Total Cost				
				CGS			
				EI			

(b) (3) LIFO

(1) Cost of Goods Sold				(2) Ending Inventory			
Date	Units	Unit Cost	Total Cost	Date	Units	Unit Cost	Total Cost

(c)

	FIFO	Average	LIFO

(d) and (e)

(a)

	FIFO	Average

(b)

(a) and (b)

General Journal

Date	Account Titles and Explanation	Ref.	Debit	Credit

P6-4A (c) to (e)	

P6-5A (a)	2004	2005
1. Cost of goods sold		
2. Net income		
3. Owner's equity		
4. Ending inventory		
5. Inventory turnover		

(b)

(a) (incorrect)

	2003	2004	2005

(a) (correct)

	2003	2004	2005

(b) and (c)

Section

Date

(a)

	PepsiCo Inc.	
	2002	2001
Inventory turnover		
Days sales in inventory		
Current ratio		
Gross profit margin		
Profit margin		

	Coca-Cola Company	
	2002	2001
Inventory turnover		
Days sales in inventory		
Current ratio		
Gross profit margin		
Profit margin		

(b)

(a) FIFO

Date	Purchases Units	Purchases Cost	Purchases Total	Cost of Goods Sold Units	Cost of Goods Sold Cost	Cost of Goods Sold Total	Balance Units	Balance Cost	Balance Total

(a) Average Cost

Date	Purchases Units	Purchases Cost	Purchases Total	Cost of Goods Sold Units	Cost of Goods Sold Cost	Cost of Goods Sold Total	Balance Units	Balance Cost	Balance Total

(a) LIFO

Date	Purchases Units	Purchases Cost	Purchases Total	Cost of Goods Sold Units	Cost of Goods Sold Cost	Cost of Goods Sold Total	Balance Units	Balance Cost	Balance Total

*P6-8A (b)	FIFO	Average	LIFO
(c)			

*P6-9A

(a) (1) FIFO

Date	Purchases			Cost of Goods Sold			Balance		
	Units	Cost	Total	Units	Cost	Total	Units	Cost	Total

(a) (2) Average Cost

Date	Purchases			Cost of Goods Sold			Balance		
	Units	Cost	Total	Units	Cost	Total	Units	Cost	Total

(b)

General Journal

Date	Account Titles and Explanation	Ref.	(1) FIFO		(2) Average	
			Dr.	Cr.	Dr.	Cr.

*P6-9A (c)   FIFO   Average

(d) and (e)

*P6-10A

(a) Average Cost - Perpetual

	Purchases			Cost of Goods Sold			Balance		
Date	Units	Cost	Total	Units	Cost	Total	Units	Cost	Total

(b)

General Journal

Date	Account Titles and Explanation	Ref.	Debit	Credit

(c)

(d) Average Cost - Periodic

Cost of Goods Sold Available for Sale					Units	Wt. Ave. Unit Cost	Total Cost
Date	Units	Unit Cost	Total Cost					
					Cost of goods sold			
					Ending inventory			

(d) (Continued)

General Journal

Date	Account Titles and Explanation	Ref.	Debit	Credit

(e)

	Perpetual		Periodic	
	Ending Inventory	Cost of Goods Sold	Ending Inventory	Cost of Goods Sold
Average cost				

(a)	Cost	Retail

(b)	

(a) and (b)

(c)

(a)

(b) (1) FIFO

(1) Cost of Goods Sold				(2) Ending Inventory			
Date	Units	Unit Cost	Total Cost	Date	Units	Unit Cost	Total Cost

(b) (2) Average Cost

(1) Cost of Goods Sold				(2) Ending Inventory			
Date	Units	Unit Cost	Total Cost	Date	Units	Unit Cost	Total Cost

(b) (3) LIFO

(1) Cost of Goods Sold				(2) Ending Inventory			
Date	Units	Unit Cost	Total Cost	Date	Units	Unit Cost	Total Cost

Section

Date

P6-2B (c)

	FIFO	Average	LIFO

(d) and (e)

P6-3B (a)

	FIFO	Average

(b)

(a) and (b)

General Journal

Date	Account Titles and Explanation	Ref.	Debit	Credit

P6-4B (c) FIFO

Cost of Goods Sold				Ending Inventory			
Date	Units	Unit Cost	Total Cost	Date	Units	Unit Cost	Total Cost

(d) and (e)

P6-5B (a)

	2004	2005
1. Cost of goods sold		
2. Net income		
3. Owner's equity		
4. Ending inventory		
5. Inventory turnover		

(b)

(a) (incorrect)

	2003	2004	2005

(a) (correct)

	2003	2004	2005

(b) and (c)

(a)	Inventory Turnover	Days Sales in Inventory	Current Ratio
2002			
2001			

(b)

(a) FIFO

	Purchases			Cost of Goods Sold			Balance		
Date	Units	Cost	Total	Units	Cost	Total	Units	Cost	Total

(a) Average Cost

	Purchases			Cost of Goods Sold			Balance		
Date	Units	Cost	Total	Units	Cost	Total	Units	Cost	Total

(a) (Continued) LIFO

Date	Purchases Units	Purchases Cost	Purchases Total	Cost of Goods Sold Units	Cost of Goods Sold Cost	Cost of Goods Sold Total	Balance Units	Balance Cost	Balance Total

(b)   FIFO   Average   LIFO

(c)

(a) (1) FIFO

Date	Purchases			Cost of Goods Sold			Balance		
	Units	Cost	Total	Units	Cost	Total	Units	Cost	Total

(a) (2) Average Cost

Date	Purchases			Cost of Goods Sold			Balance		
	Units	Cost	Total	Units	Cost	Total	Units	Cost	Total

(b)

			(1) FIFO		(2) Average	
			General Journal			
Date	Account Titles and Explanation	Ref.	Dr.	Cr.	Dr.	Cr.

*P6-9B (c)   FIFO   Average

(d) and (e)

*P6-10B

(a) FIFO - Perpetual

Date	Purchases			Cost of Goods Sold			Balance		
	Units	Cost	Total	Units	Cost	Total	Units	Cost	Total

(b)

General Journal

Date	Account Titles and Explanation	Ref.	Debit	Credit

(c)

(d) FIFO - Periodic

Cost of Goods Sold				Ending Inventory			
Date	Units	Unit Cost	Total Cost	Date	Units	Unit Cost	Total Cost

(d) (Continued)

General Journal

Date	Account Titles and Explanation	Ref.	Debit	Credit

(e)

	Perpetual		Periodic	
	Ending Inventory	Cost of Goods Sold	Ending Inventory	Cost of Goods Sold
FIFO				

(a)

	Clothing		Jewellery and Cosmetics	
	Cost	Retail	Cost	Retail

(b)

(a)	Cost	Retail

(b)	

(c)		

(d)

(a) and (c)

(a) FIFO

	Purchases			Cost of Goods Sold			Balance		
Date	Units	Cost	Total	Units	Cost	Total	Units	Cost	Total

(c) Average Cost

	Purchases			Cost of Goods Sold			Balance		
Date	Units	Cost	Total	Units	Cost	Total	Units	Cost	Total

(b) FIFO

General Journal

Date	Account Titles and Explanation	Ref.	Debit	Credit

Section _____

Date _____

(d) Average Cost

General Journal

Date	Account Titles and Explanation	Ref.	Debit	Credit

(e)

E7-1

E7-2	(a)		(b)
Procedure	Weakness	Principle Violated	Recommended Change
1.			
2.			
3.			
4.			
5.			
6.			

(a)

(b)

MEMORANDUM

TO: _____

FROM: _____

SUBJECT: _____

DATE: _____

E7-11

E7-12

(a) Internal Control Principles	Application to Cash Receipts

(b)

(d)

YAP CO.
Bank Reconciliation
March 31, 2005

(e)

General Journal

Date	Account Titles and Explanation	Ref.	Debit	Credit

(a)

(b)

MALONEY COMPANY

Bank Reconciliation

November 30, 2005

P7-6A (c)

General Journal

Date	Account Titles and Explanation	Ref.	Debit	Credit

P7-7A (a)

(b)

(c)

General Journal

Date	Account Titles and Explanation	Ref.	Debit	Credit

(d)

(a)

(b) to (c)

(a)

(b) to (c)

Internal Control Principles	Application to Cash Disbursements

(a)

General Journal

Date	Account Titles and Explanation	Ref.	Debit	Credit

(b)

Petty Cash

Date	Explanation	Ref.	Debit	Credit	Balance

(c)

P7-5B (c)

General Journal

Date	Account Titles and Explanation	Ref.	Debit	Credit

P7-6B (a)

P7-6B (b)

RIVER ADVENTURES COMPANY

Bank Reconciliation

May 31, 2005

P7-6B (c)

General Journal

Date	Account Titles and Explanation	Ref.	Debit	Credit

P7-7B (a)

(b)

(c)

General Journal

Date	Account Titles and Explanation	Ref.	Debit	Credit

(d)

(a)

CAREFREE COMPANY
Bank Reconciliation
March 31, 2005

(b)

General Journal

Date	Account Titles and Explanation	Ref.	Debit	Credit

(c)

Name

Section

Date

(a)

(b)

Part 1

Part 2 (a)

(b)

General Journal

Date	Account Titles and Explanation	Ref.	Debit	Credit

(c)

	General Journal			
Date	Account Titles and Explanation	Ref.	Debit	Credit

General Journal				
Date	Account Titles and Explanation	Ref.	Debit	Credit

(a)

General Journal

Date	Account Titles and Explanation	Ref.	Debit	Credit

(b)

General Journal

Date	Account Titles and Explanation	Ref.	Debit	Credit

(c)

General Journal

Date	Account Titles and Explanation	Ref.	Debit	Credit

(d)

General Journal

Date	Account Titles and Explanation	Ref.	Debit	Credit

(a)

General Journal

Date	Account Titles and Explanation	Ref.	Debit	Credit

(b)

General Journal

Date	Account Titles and Explanation	Ref.	Debit	Credit

Name

Section

Date

(c)

General Journal

Date	Account Titles and Explanation	Ref.	Debit	Credit

(d)

General Journal

Date	Account Titles and Explanation	Ref.	Debit	Credit

	General Journal			
Date	Account Titles and Explanation	Ref.	Debit	Credit

Name _____

Section _____

Date _____

	General Journal			
Date	Account Titles and Explanation	Ref.	Debit	Credit

Name _____

Section _____

Date _____

	General Journal			
Date	Account Titles and Explanation	Ref.	Debit	Credit

	General Journal			
Date	Account Titles and Explanation	Ref.	Debit	Credit

PB-2 Concluded

General Journal

Date	Account Titles and Explanation	Ref.	Debit	Credit

PB-3

General Journal

Date	Account Titles and Explanation	Ref.	Debit	Credit

General Journal				
Date	Account Titles and Explanation	Ref.	Debit	Credit

BEC-1 (a) Accounts Receivable Subsidiary Ledger

Duffy Co.

Date	Explanation	Ref.	Debit	Credit	Balance

Hanson Inc.

Date	Explanation	Ref.	Debit	Credit	Balance

Lewis Co.

Date	Explanation	Ref.	Debit	Credit	Balance

BEC-1 (b) General Ledger

Accounts Receivable

Date	Explanation	Ref.	Debit	Credit	Balance

BEC-2		
1.	4.	
2.	5.	
3.	6.	

BEC-3		
1.	5.	
2.	6.	
3.	7.	
4.	8.	

BEC-4	(a) Journal	(b) Journal Columns
1.		
2.		
3.		
4.		
5.		
6.		
7.		
8.		
9.		

BEC-5	Journal	Column Titles
1.		
2.		
3.		
4.		
5.		
6.		
7.		
8.		

EC-1			
1.		7.	
2.		8.	
3.		9.	
4.		10.	
5.		11.	
6.		12.	

EC-2 (a) and (b)

SING TAO COMPANY

Sales Journal S1

Date	Account Debited	Invoice No.	Ref.	Accounts Receivable Dr. Sales Cr.	Cost of Goods Sold Dr. Merch. Inventory Cr.

EC-2 (a) and (c)

SING TAO COMPANY

Purchases Journal P1

Date	Account Credited	Terms	Ref.	Merchandise Inventory Dr. Accounts Payable Cr.

EC-3 (a) and (b)

SING TAO COMPANY

Cash Receipts Journal CR1

Date	Account Credited	Ref.	Cash Dr.	Accounts Receivable Cr.	Sales Cr.	CGS Dr. Merch. Inventory Cr.	Other Accounts Cr.

(a) and (c)

SING TAO COMPANY

Cash Payments Journal   CP1

Date	Ch. No.	Payee	Cash Cr.	Merch. Inventory Dr.	Accounts Payable Dr.	Account Debited	Ref.	Other Accounts Dr.

(a) and (d)   J1

General Journal

Date	Account Titles and Explanation	Ref.	Debit	Credit

(a)

General Journal

Date	Account Titles and Explanation	Ref.	Debit	Credit

(b)

To:

From:

Subject:

EC-5

EC-6 (a) and (b)

General Ledger

Accounts Receivable

Date	Explanation	Ref.	Debit	Credit	Balance
Sept. 1	Balance				11,960

Accounts Receivable Subsidiary Ledger

Bickford

Date	Explanation	Ref.	Debit	Credit	Balance
Sept. 1	Balance				4,820

(a) and (b) (Continued)

Cavanaugh

Date	Explanation	Ref.	Debit	Credit	Balance
Sept. 1	Balance				2,060

Iman

Date	Explanation	Ref.	Debit	Credit	Balance

Jana

Date	Explanation	Ref.	Debit	Credit	Balance
Sept. 1	Balance				2,440

Kingston

Date	Explanation	Ref.	Debit	Credit	Balance
Sept. 1	Balance				2,640

(c)

PIRIE COMPANY
Schedule of Customers
September 30, 2005

	.

EC-7 (a) and (b)

SING TAO COMPANY

Sales Journal

S1

Date	Account Debited	Invoice No.	Ref.	Accounts Receivable Dr. Sales Cr.

EC-7 (a) and (c)

SING TAO COMPANY

Purchases Journal

P1

Date	Account Credited	Terms	Ref.	Purchases Dr. Accounts Payable Cr.

EC-8 (a) and (b)

SING TAO COMPANY

Cash Receipts Journal

CR1

Date	Account Credited	Ref.	Cash Dr.	Accounts Receivable Cr.	Sales Cr.	Other Accounts Cr.

EC-8 (a) and (c)

SING TAO COMPANY

Cash Payments Journal

CP1

Date	Ch. No.	Payee	Cash Cr.	Accounts Payable Dr.	Account Debited	Ref.	Other Accounts Dr.

(a) and (d)

General Journal   J1

Date	Account Titles and Explanation	Ref.	Debit	Credit

(a), (b) and (c)   Sales Journal   S1

Date	Account Debited	Invoice No.	Ref.	Accounts Receivable Dr. Sales Cr.	Cost of Goods Sold Dr. Merch. Inventory Cr.

Purchases Journal   P1

Date	Account Credited	Terms	Ref.	Merchandise Inventory Dr. Accounts Payable Cr.

General Journal   J1

Date	Account Titles and Explanation	Ref.	Debit	Credit

(a), (b) and (c) (Continued)

Cash Receipts Journal — CR1

Date	Account Credited	Ref.	Cash Dr.	Accounts Receivable Cr.	Sales Cr.	CGS Dr. Merch. Inv. Cr.	Other Accounts Cr.

Cash Payments Journal — CP1

Date	Ch. No.	Payee	Cash Cr.	Merch. Inventory Dr.	Accounts Payable Dr.	Account Debited	Ref.	Other Accounts Dr.

(a), (b) and (c)   Sales Journal   S1

Date	Account Debited	Invoice No.	Ref.	Accounts Receivable Dr. Sales Cr.	Cost of Goods Sold Dr. Merch. Inventory Cr.

Purchases Journal   P1

Date	Account Credited	Terms	Ref.	Merchandise Inventory Dr. Accounts Payable Cr.

Cash Receipts Journal   CR1

Date	Account Credited	Ref.	Cash Dr.	Accounts Receivable Cr.	Sales Cr.	CGS Dr. Merch. Inventory Cr.	Other Accounts Cr.

(a), (b) and (c) (Continued)

Cash Payments Journal   CP1

Date	Ch. No.	Payee	Cash Cr.	Merch. Inventory Dr.	Accounts Paybale Dr.	Account Debited	Ref.	Other Accounts Dr.

General Journal   J1

Date	Account Titles and Explanation	Ref.	Debit	Credit

(b)   Sales Journal   S1

Date	Account Debited	Invoice No.	Ref.	Accounts Receivable Dr. Sales Cr.	Cost of Goods Sold Dr. Merch. Inventory Cr.

Purchases Journal   P1

Date	Account Credited	Terms	Ref.	Merchandise Inventory Dr. Accounts Payable Cr.

Cash Receipts Journal   CR1

Date	Account Credited	Ref.	Cash Dr.	Accounts Receivable Cr.	Sales Cr.	CGS Dr. Merch. Inventory Cr.	Other Accounts Cr.

(b) (Continued)

Cash Payments Journal   CP1

Date	Ch. No.	Payee	Cash Cr.	Merch. Inventory Dr.	Accounts Payable Dr.	Account Debited	Ref.	Other Accounts Dr.

General Journal   J1

Date	Account Titles and Explanation	Ref.	Debit	Credit

(a) and (c)

General Ledger

Cash   No. 101

Date	Explanation	Ref.	Debit	Credit	Balance
Jan. 1	Balance				49,500

Accounts Receivable   No. 112

Date	Explanation	Ref.	Debit	Credit	Balance
Jan. 1	Balance				15,000

Notes Receivable   No. 115

Date	Explanation	Ref.	Debit	Credit	Balance
Jan. 1	Balance				45,000

Merchandise Inventory   No. 120

Date	Explanation	Ref.	Debit	Credit	Balance
Jan. 1	Balance				22,000

Land   No. 140

Date	Explanation	Ref.	Debit	Credit	Balance
Jan. 1	Balance				25,000

(a) and (c) (Continued)

Building   No. 145

Date	Explanation	Ref.	Debit	Credit	Balance
Jan. 1	Balance				75,000

Accumulated Amortization - Building   No. 146

Date	Explanation	Ref.	Debit	Credit	Balance
Jan. 1	Balance				18,000

Equipment   No. 157

Date	Explanation	Ref.	Debit	Credit	Balance
Jan. 1	Balance				6,450

Accumulated Amortization - Equipment   No. 158

Date	Explanation	Ref.	Debit	Credit	Balance
Jan. 1	Balance				1,500

Notes Payable   No. 200

Date	Explanation	Ref.	Debit	Credit	Balance

Accounts Payable   No. 201

Date	Explanation	Ref.	Debit	Credit	Balance
Jan. 1	Balance				42,000

(a) and (c) (Continued)

Mortgage Payable No. 275

Date	Explanation	Ref.	Debit	Credit	Balance
Jan. 1	Balance				82,000

M. Gibbs, Capital No. 301

Date	Explanation	Ref.	Debit	Credit	Balance
Jan. 1	Balance				94,450

M. Gibbs, Drawings No. 310

Date	Explanation	Ref.	Debit	Credit	Balance

Sales No. 401

Date	Explanation	Ref.	Debit	Credit	Balance

Sales Returns and Allowances No. 410

Date	Explanation	Ref.	Debit	Credit	Balance

Cost of Goods Sold No. 505

Date	Explanation	Ref.	Debit	Credit	Balance

Salaries Expense No. 725

Date	Explanation	Ref.	Debit	Credit	Balance

(a) and (c) (Continued)

Interest Revenue   No. 810

Date	Explanation	Ref.	Debit	Credit	Balance

Loss - Damaged Inventory   No. 920

Date	Explanation	Ref.	Debit	Credit	Balance

Accounts Receivable Subsidiary Ledger

S. Armstrong

Date	Explanation	Ref.	Debit	Credit	Balance
Jan. 1	Balance				4,500

R. Christof

Date	Explanation	Ref.	Debit	Credit	Balance
Jan. 1	Balance				3,000

B. Hibberd

Date	Explanation	Ref.	Debit	Credit	Balance
Jan. 1	Balance				7,500

B. Rhol

Date	Explanation	Ref.	Debit	Credit	Balance

(a) and (c) (Continued)

Accounts Payable Subsidiary Ledger

Fieldstone Corp.

Date	Explanation	Ref.	Debit	Credit	Balance
Jan. 1	Balance				9,000

Harms Distributors

Date	Explanation	Ref.	Debit	Credit	Balance
Jan. 1	Balance				16,000

Lapeska Co.

Date	Explanation	Ref.	Debit	Credit	Balance
Jan. 1	Balance				1,900

Warren Parts Co.

Date	Explanation	Ref.	Debit	Credit	Balance

Watson & Co.

Date	Explanation	Ref.	Debit	Credit	Balance
Jan. 1					17,000

(d)

	Debit	Credit

(e)

(b)   Sales Journal   S1

Date	Account Debited	Invoice No.	Ref.	Accounts Receivable Dr. Sales Cr.	CGS Dr. Merch. Inventory Cr.

Purchases Journal   P1

Date	Account Credited	Terms	Ref.	Merchandise Inventory Dr. Accounts Payable Cr.

General Journal   J1

Date	Account Titles and Explanation	Ref.	Debit	Credit

Cash Receipts Journal   CR1

Date	Account Credited	Ref.	Cash Dr.	Accounts Receivable Cr.	Sales Cr.	CGS Dr. Merch. Inventory Cr.	Other Accounts Cr.

(b) (Continued)

Cash Payments Journal CP1

Date	Ch. No.	Payee	Cash Cr.	Merch. Inventory Dr.	Accounts Payable Dr.	Account Debited	Ref.	Other Accounts Dr.

(a) and (c)

General Ledger

Cash No. 101

Date	Explanation	Ref.	Debit	Credit	Balance
May 1	Balance				36,700

Accounts Receivable No. 112

Date	Explanation	Ref.	Debit	Credit	Balance
May 1	Balance				15,400

Notes Receivable No. 115

Date	Explanation	Ref.	Debit	Credit	Balance
May 1	Balance				48,000

(a) and (c) (Continued)

Merchandise Inventory   No. 120

Date	Explanation	Ref.	Debit	Credit	Balance
May 1	Balance				22,000

Equipment   No. 157

Date	Explanation	Ref.	Debit	Credit	Balance
May 1	Balance				8,200

Accumulated Amortization - Equipment   No. 158

Date	Explanation	Ref.	Debit	Credit	Balance
May 1	Balance				1,800

Notes Payable   No. 200

Date	Explanation	Ref.	Debit	Credit	Balance

Accounts Payable   No. 201

Date	Explanation	Ref.	Debit	Credit	Balance
May 1	Balance				43,400

C. Scholz, Capital   No. 301

Date	Explanation	Ref.	Debit	Credit	Balance
May 1	Balance				85,100

(a) and (c) (Continued)

C. Scholz, Drawings   No. 310

Date	Explanation	Ref.	Debit	Credit	Balance

Sales   No. 401

Date	Explanation	Ref.	Debit	Credit	Balance

Sales Returns and Allowances   No. 410

Date	Explanation	Ref.	Debit	Credit	Balance

Cost of Goods Sold   No. 505

Date	Explanation	Ref.	Debit	Credit	Balance

Salaries Expense   No. 725

Date	Explanation	Ref.	Debit	Credit	Balance

Rent Expense   No. 730

Date	Explanation	Ref.	Debit	Credit	Balance

Interest Revenue   No. 810

Date	Explanation	Ref.	Debit	Credit	Balance

Name _____

Section _____

Date _____

(a) and (c) (Continued)

Accounts Receivable Subsidiary Ledger

L. Cellars

Date	Explanation	Ref.	Debit	Credit	Balance
May 1	Balance				7,400

W. Karasch

Date	Explanation	Ref.	Debit	Credit	Balance
May 1	Balance				3,250

G. Parrish

Date	Explanation	Ref.	Debit	Credit	Balance
May 1	Balance				4,750

B. Simone

Date	Explanation	Ref.	Debit	Credit	Balance

Accounts Payable Subsidiary Ledger

Buttercup Distributors

Date	Explanation	Ref.	Debit	Credit	Balance
May 1	Balance				17,400

Elite Sports

Date	Explanation	Ref.	Debit	Credit	Balance
May 1	Balance				15,500

(a) and (c) (Continued)

Lancio Co.

Date	Explanation	Ref.	Debit	Credit	Balance

Werner Widgits

Date	Explanation	Ref.	Debit	Credit	Balance

Winterware Corp.

Date	Explanation	Ref.	Debit	Credit	Balance
May 1	Balance				10,500

(d)

	Debit	Credit

(e)

(a), (b) and (c)   Sales Journal   S1

Date	Account Debited	Invoice No.	Ref.	Accounts Receivable Dr. Sales Cr.

Purchases Journal   P1

Date	Account Credited	Terms	Ref.	Purchases Dr. Accounts Payable Cr.

General Journal   J1

Date	Account Titles and Explanation	Ref.	Debit	Credit

(a), (b) and (c) (Continued)

Cash Receipts Journal   CR1

Date	Account Credited	Ref.	Cash Dr.	Accounts Receivable Cr.	Sales Cr.	Other Accounts Cr.

Cash Payments Journal   CP1

Date	Ch. No.	Payee	Cash Cr.	Accounts Payable Dr.	Account Debited	Ref.	Other Accounts Dr.

(a)   Sales Journal   S1

Date	Account Debited	Invoice No.	Ref.	Accounts Receivable Dr. Sales Cr.	CGS Dr. Merch. Inventory Cr.

Purchases Journal   P1

Date	Account Credited	Terms	Ref.	Merchandise Inventory Dr. Accounts Payable Cr.

(a) (Continued)

Cash Receipts Journal

Date	Account Credited	Ref.	Cash Dr.	Accounts Receivable Cr.	Sales Cr.	CGS Dr. Merch. Inv. Cr.	Other Accounts Dr.

Cash Payments Journal

Date	Ch. No.	Payee	Cash Cr.	Merch. Inventory Dr.	Accounts Payable Dr.	Account Debited	Ref.	Other Accounts Dr.

Name

Section

Date

(a), (d) and (f)

	General Journal			J1
Date	Account Titles and Explanation	Ref.	Debit	Credit

(a), (d) and (f) (Continued)

General Journal   J2

Date	Account Titles and Explanation	Ref.	Debit	Credit

(b) and (f)

Cash   No. 101

Date	Explanation	Ref.	Debit	Credit	Balance
Jan. 1	Balance				35,050

Accounts Receivable   No. 112

Date	Explanation	Ref.	Debit	Credit	Balance
Jan. 1	Balance				14,000

Notes Receivable   No. 115

Date	Explanation	Ref.	Debit	Credit	Balance
Jan. 1	Balance				39,000

Merchandise Inventory   No. 120

Date	Explanation	Ref.	Debit	Credit	Balance
Jan. 1	Balance				20,000

Office Supplies   No. 125

Date	Explanation	Ref.	Debit	Credit	Balance
Jan. 1	Balance				1,000

(b) and (f) (Continued)

Prepaid Insurance   No. 130

Date	Explanation	Ref.	Debit	Credit	Balance
Jan. 1	Balance				2,000

Land   No. 140

Date	Explanation	Ref.	Debit	Credit	Balance
Jan. 1	Balance				50,000

Building   No. 145

Date	Explanation	Ref.	Debit	Credit	Balance
Jan. 1	Balance				100,000

Accumulated Amortization - Building   No. 146

Date	Explanation	Ref.	Debit	Credit	Balance
Jan. 1	Balance				25,000

Equipment   No. 157

Date	Explanation	Ref.	Debit	Credit	Balance
Jan. 1	Balance				6,450

Accumulated Amortization - Equipment   No. 158

Date	Explanation	Ref.	Debit	Credit	Balance
Jan. 1	Balance				1,500

Notes Payable   No. 200

Date	Explanation	Ref.	Debit	Credit	Balance

(b) and (f) (Continued)

Accounts Payable — No. 201

Date	Explanation	Ref.	Debit	Credit	Balance
Jan. 1	Balance				36,000

Interest Payable — No. 230

Date	Explanation	Ref.	Debit	Credit	Balance

Mortgage Payable — No. 275

Date	Explanation	Ref.	Debit	Credit	Balance
Jan. 1	Balance				125,000

Income Summary — No. 300

Date	Explanation	Ref.	Debit	Credit	Balance

A. Kassam, Capital — No. 301

Date	Explanation	Ref.	Debit	Credit	Balance
Jan. 1	Balance				80,000

A. Kassam, Drawings — No. 306

Date	Explanation	Ref.	Debit	Credit	Balance

(b) and (f) (Continued)

Sales   No. 401

Date	Explanation	Ref.	Debit	Credit	Balance

Sales Returns and Allowances   No. 410

Date	Explanation	Ref.	Debit	Credit	Balance

Cost of Goods Sold   No. 505

Date	Explanation	Ref.	Debit	Credit	Balance

Loss - Inventory Shrinkage   No. 506

Date	Explanation	Ref.	Debit	Credit	Balance

Amortization Expense   No. 711

Date	Explanation	Ref.	Debit	Credit	Balance

Interest Expense   No. 718

Date	Explanation	Ref.	Debit	Credit	Balance

(b) and (f) (Continued)

Insurance Expense   No. 722

Date	Explanation	Ref.	Debit	Credit	Balance

Salaries Expense   No. 725

Date	Explanation	Ref.	Debit	Credit	Balance

Office Supplies Expense   No. 728

Date	Explanation	Ref.	Debit	Credit	Balance

(b) and (f) (Continued)

Accounts Receivable Subsidiary Ledger

R. Draves

Date	Explanation	Ref.	Debit	Credit	Balance
Jan. 1	Balance				1,500

J. Ebel

Date	Explanation	Ref.	Debit	Credit	Balance

B. Jacovetti

Date	Explanation	Ref.	Debit	Credit	Balance
Jan. 1	Balance				7,500

S. Kysely

Date	Explanation	Ref.	Debit	Credit	Balance
Jan. 1	Balance				5,000

(b) and (f) (Continued)

Accounts Payable Subsidiary Ledger

Laux Supplies

Date	Explanation	Ref.	Debit	Credit	Balance

Liazuk Co.

Date	Explanation	Ref.	Debit	Credit	Balance
Jan. 1	Balance				10,000

Mikush Bros.

Date	Explanation	Ref.	Debit	Credit	Balance
Jan. 1	Balance				15,000

Nguyen & Son

Date	Explanation	Ref.	Debit	Credit	Balance
Jan. 1	Balance				11,000

Welz Wares

Date	Explanation	Ref.	Debit	Credit	Balance

Name

Section

Date

(c) and (d)

	Unadjusted		Adjusted	
	Debit	Credit	Debit	Credit

(c) (Continued)

(e)

(e) (Continued)

(g)

	Debit	Credit